The Revelation
A Historicist View

BARRY MIDYET

WESTBOW
PRESS®
A DIVISION OF THOMAS NELSON
& ZONDERVAN

WestBow Press books may be ordered through booksellers or by contacting:

WestBow Press
A Division of Thomas Nelson & Zondervan
1663 Liberty Drive
Bloomington, IN 47403
www.westbowpress.com
1 (866) 928-1240

ISBN: 978-1-5127-6336-2 (sc)

Library of Congress Control Number: 2016918493

Print information available on the last page.

WestBow Press rev. date: 3/2/2017

Introduction: A Literal Translation of Rev 1:1-3

A revelation of Jesus Christ, which God gave to Him to show to His servants things which must come to pass with speed. And He sent and signified it through His angel to His servant John ²who bore witness to the word of God and to the testimony of Jesus Christ—as many of both that he saw. ³Blessed is the one reading and the ones hearing the words of the prophecy and keeping the things written in it for the time is near.

John's Introduction to the Revelation

The Holy Bible—easily the most read book in the history of the world—is in essence the story of God's chosen people, from the coming of Adam to the coming of Jesus the much-prophesied Messiah exactly four thousand years later. But many of the Messianic prophecies—the ones saying the Messiah (or Anointed One or Christ) would become a great king—went unfulfilled when the sojourn of Jesus on Earth was cut short by His death on the cross. So it almost goes without saying that the Bible cannot end that way. Therefore, God has given us the last book of the New Testament in which the resurrected Jesus returns, as promised in the Gospels, to reveal His kingdom to John. And John recorded everything he saw and heard.

Because John calls himself a servant of Jesus and not His disciple, the identity of the author, while not questioned by the early Church, has been questioned by modern "scholars." Nonetheless, the overwhelming evidence is that the author is His beloved disciple John. In all four gospels, Jesus indicates that one or more disciples would live to see Him return; but in John's Gospel, Jesus signifies that John would be the one who would live to see Him return to reveal the Kingdom of God (see John 21:22). Church Fathers tell us that the Revelation was received in AD 95 or 96 when John was about a hundred years old.

Because the Revelation was recorded in Greek, it soon came to be known in the ancient world by its first word *Apokalupsis,* or "Apocalypse" as it is called in the West, which literally means "an unveiling" or as commonly translated, "A Revelation." In the United States it is sometimes, especially in the south, called "Revelations." But while it is true that the Revelation foretells of many events of the future, they are best thought of as a singular great story, which can best be summed up as an epic battle for the Earth that would soon be waged by the followers of Jesus.

John's title, A Revelation of Jesus Christ, emphasizes its divine source and also, like most things in the Revelation, it has a second meaning. The last book of the Bible is a Revelation of Jesus as the Christ (or Anointed One) who is to rule over all the kings of the Earth.

John immediately adds, in what could be called a subtitle, that the things in the Revelation are things "that must come to pass with speed." This is the first of two keys that must be picked up in order to unlock the mysteries of the Revelation—the other being the first vision (at the end of this chapter). The sense of immediacy is repeated often—in verse 3 by John and in verse 19 by Jesus. Upon this underlying precept, the remainder of the Revelation rests. Others may say that everything, from the arrival of the first horseman to the arrival of the fifth horseman, is to take place nineteen or twenty centuries later; but this commentary will not call Jesus and John liars. The reader is urged to keep a world history book side-by-side with this commentary in order to verify that the Revelation foretells of events that began unfolding soon after the Revelation was received. As the reader approaches the end of the Revelation, he or she is well-advised to keep an eye on the world news.

We should note that the source of the Revelation is God who is the only one who knows the future (see Matthew 24:36). God the Father revealed the future to His Son Jesus, and Jesus, in turn, signified it to His servant John through "His angel." While many angels appear in the Revelation, John clearly suggests that one angel directed the other angels, presumably the "strong angel" who first appears in chapter 5.

John, in turn, is giving to us—the rest of the servants of Jesus—an eyewitness account of all the things signified to him by Jesus and His angel. Only in the Revelation and in John's Gospel are the prophecies of Jesus said to be signified to us (see John 12:33, 18:32, 21:19 in the KJV or NKJV Bible). The Greek word *semaino* literally means "to make known with signs," and that is a fitting description of the means Jesus utilizes in the relaying of God's revelation of the future to His servant John.

While many commentaries denigrate the Revelation, insisting its theology is not found elsewhere in the Bible—and even suggesting it was written by an imposter and should be removed from the Bible—this commentary will uphold the Revelation's rightful place in the Bible and treat its words, like John says, as both the Word of God and the testimony of Jesus. Most of the first three chapters are dictated by Jesus word by word, making it truly, more-so than any other book of the Bible, the Word of God. And the fulfillment of His Word(s) is the testimony (or proof) of Jesus.

In verse 3, a blessing is promised to the reader of the Revelation who keeps it in their mind and heart, and especially remembers that the things in it were to come to pass with speed. The blessing is no doubt a greater faith in Jesus and in God; for the ultimate testimony to Jesus and to the existence of an all-knowing God, is the spirit of prophecy (as the angel tells us in 19:10).

John's wording of the promise reflects the fact that it was common practice in the first century churches for a reader to stand and read to the congregation (or the hearer) from the precious canon of scripture that each church possessed. It is hard to imagine today, but before the coming of the printing press, it was extremely rare for an individual to possess a complete copy of scripture. Moreover, many first-century Christians were illiterate, so the typical hearer could only try to memorize it as best he could. In John's choice of words, he is making it clear that he expects the Revelation to be added to the holy canon of scripture that each Church possessed. The blessing applies equally as well, if not more so, to the reader of today who typically is able to read from a personal copy of the Revelation in the comfort of his or her home until it is firmly fixed in mind and heart. But the blessing is not absolute and is conditional upon the reader or hearer keeping foremost in mind that the time of its fulfillment was near.

Salutations: A Literal Translation of Rev 1:4-8

> John to the seven churches which are in Asia: Grace to you and peace from the One who is and was, and is coming, and from the seven Spirits which are before His throne, ⁵and from Jesus Christ the faithful martyr, the firstborn of the dead, and the ruler of the kings of the earth.

> To the one who loved us and washed away our sins in His blood ⁶and made us to be kings and priests to His God and Father, to Him be the glory and dominion to the ages of the ages. Amen. ⁷Behold, He is coming with the clouds and every eye will see [the event], and those who pierced Him. And all the tribes of the earth will wail because of Him. Yes! Amen!

> ⁸I am the Alpha and Omega, the beginning and the End, says the Lord, the One who is, and was, and is coming—the Almighty.

John's Salutation

John's salutation, and the Revelation as a whole, is primarily directed to seven churches in the Roman province of Asia, which encompassed western Asia Minor and not all of Asia. Identified in verse 11 as Ephesus, Smyrna, Pergamos, Thyatira, Sardis, Philadelphia and Laodicea, they are singled out from among the many churches in Asia for a blessing of grace and peace.

A short prayer for the granting of grace and peace from God and Jesus is the usual greeting of New Testament epistles. But here the salutation is strikingly different (e.g., compare with Philippians 1:2; I Peter 1:2; & II John 3). John has done away with the usual Holy Trinity and says the blessing of grace and peace is to come from "the One who is, and was, and is coming, and from *seven Spirits* before His throne and from Jesus Christ the faithful martyr and the first-born of the dead and ruler of the kings of the Earth."

Like many things in the Revelation, the salutation is rather shocking. The concept of God the Father being the Living, Ancient, and Eternal One, and the very similar concept of God the Son being the first born of the dead (or the One who is) and the ruler over the kings of the Earth (who is Coming), can be found elsewhere in the Bible. But there is little that prepares us for the concept of seven Spirits. In the rest of the New Testament there is but one divine Spirit, usually called the Holy Spirit. But don't worry, John has not lost his marbles. He may be jumping ahead a bit, but as Jesus explains in the vision that follows (verses 12-20), the seven churches to which the Revelation is addressed are to be thought of as seven stars that point to seven Churches of the future that Jesus calls seven lamp-stand assemblies. It is best to think of the seven churches on earth (and especially their governor or king) as being the stand, and think of the seven Spirits as being the "lamps of fire" that come down from heaven and sit atop them (as signified in the second vision, in chapter 4).

A little digging into scripture reveals that the seven Spirits are also pointed to, or signified, in the Old Testament. That is, in Exodus, they are incorporated into the ancient Israelites' Tabernacle of God—and later into King Solomon's Temple—in the form of seven golden lamps burning before the Holy of Holies—God's throne—just as in the Revelation they are also seen as seven lamps of fire burning before God's throne (compare Revelation 4:5 to Exodus 25:37). Later in the Old Testament, when Solomon's temple was being rebuilt by Zerubbabel, the prophet Zechariah was speaking of the seven Spirits when he said, "These seven rejoice to see the plumb line in the hand of Zerubbabel. They are the eyes of the Lord which scan to and fro throughout the whole Earth" (Zechariah 4:10). In summary, John's salutation to the seven Asian churches is looking forward to the future when seven Spirits will give light to the seven parts of the Earth. They are also the eyes of God, through which He judges us.

In verses 5b-7, John salutes Jesus who has done two things for us. (1) He washed away our sins in His blood that He shed on the cross for us—an event that lies at the heart of Christianity but is only recorded in John's Gospel (see John 19).

(2) He is to make us His kings and priests at His second coming which every eye would see. It should be noted here that, while some faulty Bibles (based on the NU text) say "made us to be a kingdom" (which implies that there will be only one kingdom and Jesus will be the king), the Received Text clearly says "made us to be kings" indicating many kingdoms.

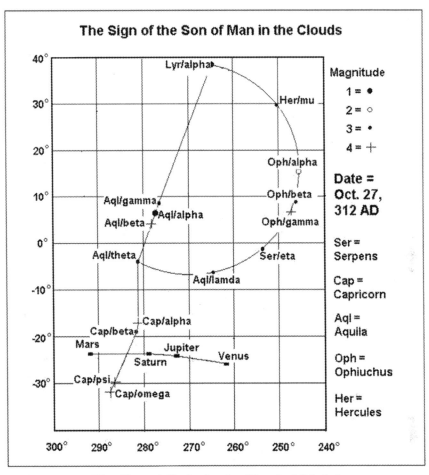

The Sign of Christ in the Clouds (chi-rho)

In AD 312, every eye did indeed see the second coming of Jesus as the Christ (i.e., the advent of Christendom). That is, every eye saw the sign of Christ in the clouds (a chi-rho, the first two letters of Christ in Greek) on October 27th when also Jesus appeared to St. Constantine and said, "By this, conquer." If it was too cloudy, they soon saw it on all Roman armor, on Roman coins, and prominently displayed in all Churches. It was a very rare alignment of the planets Mars, Saturn, Jupiter and Venus like four ducks in a row that formed an X with four stars in Capricorn, and the P is always there.[1]

It brought judgment day for the sixth head of Satan (i.e., pagan Rome and the pagan Roman soldiers who pierced Him). In the history books, that day is known as the turning point of history because, ever since that day, Christian nations have been the dominant force on Earth.[2] Or as the Revelation puts it, many pagan rulers (and soldiers) have wailed since that day. The five horsemen of the Revelation can be thought of as five dispensations of the second coming, which allow Christians to rule the Earth to the end despite Satan's best attempts to thwart it.

5

It should be noted here that there is no way, despite what many futurists may say, that verse 7 can refer to the future (our future) because pagan Rome, and pagan Roman soldiers, no longer exist.

1. Source: *Distant Suns*, Ver. 2 (a star-tracking program for PCs)
2. That is, all world history textbooks used to say that (back when they actually stuck to historical facts). But history has been completely rewritten in modern textbooks so as not to offend atheists, Muslims, Buddhists, etc. Nonetheless, there are a few historians who still say the same thing. For example, Robert Thorvat says,

> On the 28th of October, AD 312, Constantine The Great "faced off" with Maxentius in what became known as the Battle of the Milvian Bridge. Though no one probably realized this at the time, the Battle of the Milvian Bridge would become one of those historical turning points that would set world history down a new path whether for better or worse.

(Source: https://roberthorvat30.wordpress.com/2013/10/28/the-battle-of-the-milvian-bridge-on-this-day-in-history/)

Salutation of Jesus

Jesus is the speaker in verse 8. Alpha and Omega is the beginning and the end of the Greek alphabet, the common language of the day. Jesus means that He, like God, is eternal, and He was present at the beginning as John also says in his Gospel (see John 1:1-2) and He will still be with us at the end.

The Setting: A Literal Translation of Rev 1:9-11

> I, John, both your brother and companion in the tribulation, and in the kingdom and endurance of Jesus Christ, was on the Isle called Patmos because of the word of God and because of the testimony of Jesus Christ. [10]I was in [the] spirit on the Lord's Day, and heard behind me a great voice as of a trumpet, [11]saying, I am the Alpha and the Omega, the first and the last; what you see, write in a scroll and send to the seven churches which are in Asia: to Ephesus, and to Smyrna, and to Pergamos, and to Thyatira, and to Sardis, and to Philadelphia, and to Laodicea.

The "Theometric" Setting of the Revelation

Verse 9 reflects the state of Christendom near the end of the first century. The tribulation John refers to is the persecution suffered by the Church during the reign of Domitian, who was the first Roman emperor to order everyone to worship him as a God, which Christians refused to do.

Jerome tells us that Domitian banished John to a penal colony/mining camp on the Isle of Patmos shortly after he came to power, and John remained there until Domitian's death in AD 96. One of the first things a visitor notices, when visiting the Isle of Patmos today, is that the small L-shaped Island is pit-marked throughout with thousands of caves and mines. Being a mine worker is a tough job at any age, so it seems almost incredible that an old man like John was working and living in a Patmos penal colony. But that is the inescapable picture being painted, for John surely had to be perceived as a threat to Rome as he hated pagan Rome and yearned for the advent of Christendom. On the positive side, busting rocks and/or keeping the furnaces fired likely helped John remain healthy and robust well into his nineties.

On a second level, if not the first, the poetic prose of verse 9 suggests (or signifies) that the real reason for John being on the Isle of Patmos was not a result of happenstance or bad luck, but for Jesus to be able to present him with the Revelation, which is both the Word of God and the testimony (or proof) of Jesus. The location of John is in fact very crucial to the Revelation as is the location of the Asian churches to which it is addressed. There is no word for it, but the location(s) of John and the seven Asian churches are integral parts of what could be called the "theometrics" woven into the Revelation. That is, in the setting, Jesus has woven advanced spherical geometry into the Revelation as the ultimate testimony to its divine source. The result is a strikingly beautiful dove-shaped "starguide" that guides the reader to the seven golden lampstands of the Church that in turn form a sharp two two-edged sword. And the dove is shaped like an arrow that points to the Isle of Patmos and (theoretically) to the spot where John received the Revelation. Also, the mid-point between the arrow and the location of John marks the center of the sword (theoretically, but it will take advanced software to prove it). The starguide also guides the reader (or at least today's reader who has access to a PC that plots Great Circles) to every good thing foretold in the Revelation even if it's on the other side of the world.

Moreover, besides John having to be exactly where he was, John had to be there exactly *when* he was. It is evident from the prophesies in the Gospels, foretelling of Jesus revealing the Kingdom of God to John, that Jesus knew it would not be possible to return with it until John was old and had outlived the other disciples (e.g., see John 21:20-22). There is a compelling reason for Jesus having to delay His return for more than sixty years. If He had come earlier, several integral parts of the all-important setting of the Revelation would not have existed. That is, several of the seven churches of the Asian starguide are not mentioned elsewhere in the Bible, and neither are they mentioned in any other writings before the early second century; so it is very likely that they did not exist before the late first century.

John says the return of Jesus came to pass when he was "in spirit on the Lord's Day." This is the first recorded reference to "the Lord's Day." There is some debate, but the evidence points to the "Lord's Day" as being Sunday, the first day of the week. That is, we are not told in the Bible that Jesus specifically told His followers to do so, but historians attest that after His resurrection from the dead (which occurred on Sunday), His followers began assembling together on Sunday morning to commemorate the event—as we are also told in Acts 20:7 and Corinthians 16:2.

It can also be argued that, while John was a Christian, he was also a Jew and long accustomed to worshipping God on the Sabbath Day, i.e., Saturday. The Bible confirms that many Jewish Christians did indeed continue to worship God on Saturday for a while (see Acts 13:14, 13:42, 44; 17:2, 18:4). Even so, there is no reason to doubt that, in time, all of the Jewish Christians also met on Sunday. Church historians tell us that the practice of also meeting on Saturday began to die out in the late first century, but not entirely. (On a personal note, my great-grandfather—who was both a Christian and a Jew—went to the synagogue on Saturday and to church on Sunday, as did my grandfather until he married grandma and she nixed that family tradition). In AD 325, Constantine convened all the leaders of the Church together to settle all such theological matters, and Sunday was declared to be the Lord's Day and the day for believers to mass for communion and to worship the Lord Jesus.

The meaning of "in spirit" has been much debated. John's use of the phrase is unique to the Revelation where it is found four times (also see Revelation 4:2; 17:3 and 21:10). The Greek word for spirit is *pneuma*, which means anything invisible, from the invisible wind to the invisible Spirit of God. So we must take a close look at the context and the syntax. Although a "the" is usually added by translators, which tends to suggest the Holy Spirit, the original Greek has no such "the" before spirit, so it is best left un-capitalized as is typical in the other three cases (see Revelation 4:2; 17:3 & 21:10 in the KJV Bible).

The context suggests that John was deep in thought or meditating on the words of his beloved Lord. To speculate a bit on what John may have been in deep thought about, one oft-recurring thought had to be the words of Jesus to Peter indicating that he, John, would not taste death before seeing His blessed Lord return (see John 21:23). That is, he probably thought quite often about the inescapable fact that he was in his late nineties, his strength waning, and that Rome might soon work him to his death if His Lord were to delay His return any longer. Or he may have been in prayer about it, or perhaps conducting a worship service as some commentaries suggest. Whatever the case, John is startled to his senses by a loud voice behind him that sounded like a trumpet.

The booming voice behind John tells him to record whatever he sees and send it to seven churches in Asia Minor. The Received Text tells us that the speaker introduces Himself first, saying, "I am the Alpha and Omega, the first and the last." That is of course the same title of Jesus in verse 8 (in the received Greek text). In contrast, the NU and M Greek Texts do not have the voice identifying itself at this point at all. The differences have led to some doubt as to who the speaker is. An underlying assumption of this commentary is that the booming voice comes from Jesus *en persona*; and being God made flesh, Jesus is right in calling himself the Alpha and Omega, the first and the last (see commentary on verse 8).

The churches in the Roman province of Asia to which Jesus directs the Revelation are mentioned often, so the significance of the cities of Ephesus, Smyrna, Pergamos, Thyatira, Sardis, Philadelphia, and Laodicea must not be underestimated. As shown on the cover, by connecting the cities in the order given, they form a perfect outline of a dove. The dove is perfect because the area encompassed by the left wing is equal to the size of the right wing—making the dove a perfectly symmetrical geometric figure. The dove is also the traditional symbol of the Holy Spirit, one of whose jobs is to "announce things to come" (John 16:13). The seven Asian cities are called stars and messengers in verse 20. So we can conclude that they are to be utilized as seven star-like messengers that form a total of 21 vectors which guide the reader to all the good things that are foretold in the otherwise very mysterious Revelation.

The First Vision: A Literal Translation of Rev 1:12-20

> And I turned to see the voice that spoke with me. And having turned I saw seven golden lampstands, ¹³and in the midst of the seven lampstands One like the Son of Man, clothed with a garment down to the feet and girded about the chest with a golden band. ¹⁴His head and hair were white like wool, as white as snow, and His eyes like a flame of fire. ¹⁵His feet were like fine brass, as if refined in a furnace, and His voice as the sound of many waters. ¹⁶He had in His right hand seven stars, out of His mouth went a sharp two-edged sword, and His countenance was like the sun shining in its strength. ¹⁷And when I saw Him, I fell at His feet as dead. But He laid His right hand on me, saying to me, Do not be afraid. I am the First and the Last; ¹⁸I am He who lives, and was dead, and behold, I am alive forevermore. Amen. And I have the keys of Hades and of Death. ¹⁹Write the things which you have seen, and the things which are, and the things which will take place after this. ²⁰The mystery of the seven stars which you saw in My right hand, and the seven golden lampstands: The seven stars are the messengers of the seven churches, and the seven lampstands which you saw are seven churches.

The Map of the World

After hearing a loud voice, John turns and sees seven golden lampstands and Jesus standing in the middle of them. He is in His "transfigured" body, first seen in the Gospels (see Matthew 17). John's description of the feet of Jesus reflects the fact that John had first-hand knowledge about refining brass. Sitting in the right hand of Jesus are seven stars, and in His mouth was a sharp two-edged sword.

John apparently faints from fear, and Jesus lets go of the stars and lays His right hand on John and comforts him, and then adds "I am the First and the Last … who lives, and was dead, and behold, I am alive forevermore. And I have the keys of Hades and of Death." As in verse 11, Jesus again says He is the First and the Last, but this time he adds that He has the keys to Hades and death (or hell and death). Preachers nowadays only like to talk about the love of God, but half of the Bible is about the wrath of God.

In verse 19 we are told that the vision is of "things which are" and "things that will take place after this." The seven stars are clearly "the things which are," and that leaves the seven golden lampstands as "the things that will take place after this."

The seven stars and seven golden lampstands are interpreted by Jesus in verse 20. The seven stars are the seven Asian churches of verse 11. As for the identity of the golden lampstands, Jesus, in the original Greek, makes it clear that the lampstands are NOT the seven churches in Asia because He does not put a "the" in front of Churches in the second key to the mystery. Besides, it almost goes without saying that the seven Asian churches cannot be in two places at the same time. To see what happens to translators who add to the Revelation, see Rev 22:18.

It should be noted that the seven Asian churches are on the right hand of Jesus, meaning Jesus is facing north, the orientation of all world maps (or any map), and that they are called stars and messengers. We are to navigate the Revelation with them, just as a sailor navigates the dark scary sea by observing the seven brightest stars.

A little investigation into the vision reveals that the coordinates of seven Asian churches serve as seven star-like messengers that form twenty-one vectors that point to many good things that have occurred since the Revelation was written. Seven of the vectors point to the seven golden lampstands of the Church—the seven Patriarchates of the Church established by the early Church with the help of the Christian Emperors that resulted from the second coming of Jesus (in AD 312). They were established to bring light to the seven parts of the Earth. They are the Churches of Rome, Jerusalem, Antioch, Alexandria, Constantinople, Turnovo and Pec. To see which stars point to them, see the cover of this book. When connected on a world map or globe, they resemble a sharp two-edged sword (or dagger) used by soldiers in the first century.

It should also be noted that, even when they are a hundred miles apart, the vectors point to both the lamp and stand, i.e., to the throne of the Patriarch of the Church and to the throne of the king or governor whose main purpose, according to the Revelation, is to protect the Church from harm and to conquer on behalf of the Church. (And current kings, presidents, prime ministers, etc. should take note of that).

The sword in the mouth of Jesus primarily represents the word of God (see Hebrews 4:12). But like most things in the Revelation, it has a second meaning. That is, Jesus, and/or His mouth, helps mark the center point of the sharp two-edged sword formed by the seven golden lampstands. In mathematical terms, where He is standing is one of the two foci that mark the center of the sharp two-edged sword. The other foci is the seven stars, presumably the center of them. The point halfway between the two foci is the center of the vision. The spot where Jesus is standing also marks the spot where John sealed up the seven thunders (in chapter 10). They are no doubt meant to be found by someone in our day—either by someone equipped with a GPS connected to a powerful computer that is able to provide the exact spot, or else by someone taking a far easier route, taking the Church's word for it. According to the Orthodox Church, Jesus was standing just outside a cave known today as the Cave of the Apocalypse, where John is said to have lived and where he wrote the Revelation. A rough, low-tech calculation made with a ruler and a World Atlas reveals that the Church may be quite right. The catch is, the cave is the second holiest site in Greece and is guarded 24/7 by monks who are not inclined to let just anyone come in and start poking around.

The scale of the vision appears to be 1 cubit (half the length of a man's arm or about half a meter) = 250 furlongs (about 50 kilometers) or a ratio of 1:100,000.

Here are the the coordinates of the seven stars so the inquisitive reader can plug them into his or her computer and see for themselves what they point to (from Biblestudy.org):

Ephesus: 37.941111 N, 27.341944 E
Smyrna: 38.418611 N, 27.139167 E
Pergamos: 39.1325 N, 27.184167 E
Thyatira: 38.920833 N, 27.841667 E
Sardis: 38.488333 N, 28.040278 E
Philadelphia: 38.35 N, 28.516667 E
Laodicea: 37.835833 N, 29.1075 E

(I am in the process of creating an appendix that lists the hundreds of cities and battlefields, etc. that are pointed to by the 21 vectors of the starguide, but it won't be ready by the time this book goes to print. So I plan to post it at some point on my website, 7stars7lamstands.com).

To summarize the first vision, the star-like coordinates of the seven churches in Asia Minor form 21 vectors which can be extended into great circles that go around the Earth, and they accurately guide the reader to every good thing foretold in the Revelation. There is also a "bad" vector, introduced later, that guides the reader to the demon-possessed kings of the East who start the Battle of Ar Mageddon. That means pretty much any proposed interpretation of anything in the Revelation can easily be proven or disproven by the advanced spherical geometry Jesus has woven into the Revelation for today's sleuths. Therefore, there is very little in this commentary on the Revelation that cannot be conclusively proven with the vectors Jesus has woven into it.

The Seven Letters

A Literal Translation of Rev 2:1-7

To the messenger of the church of Ephesus write, These things says the One holding the seven stars on His right [hand], and who walks in the middle of the seven golden lampstands. ²I know your works, and your labor and your endurance. And I know you cannot tolerate evil. And you tested those who say they are apostles and are not, and found them liars. ³And you have borne and endured and labored for My name's sake and not grown weary.

⁴Yet I hold this against you: that you have forsaken your first love. ⁵Remember therefore from where you have fallen, and repent, and do the first works. Else I am coming to you quickly, and I will remove your lampstand out of its place unless you repent.

⁶But this you have, that you hate the practices of the Nicolaitans which I also hate.

⁷The one having an ear, let it hear what the Spirit says to the Churches: To the One that conquers I will give to it to eat of the tree of life which is in the middle of the Paradise of God.

The Letter to Ephesus

This is the first of seven timely and prophetic letters from Jesus to the seven Asian churches, or more correctly, to the seven messengers of the seven churches. The messengers are also called stars (see Rev 1:20), and each star/messenger is synonymous with one of the Asian churches to which the entire Revelation is sent (see 1:11). And each of the star/messengers, we can glean from the first vision, form vectors with the other star/messengers which point to, and forward the letters to, the seven golden lampstands of the Church that would soon be established and that Jesus is walking in the middle of. It follows then that the seven letters are directed not to the Asian churches *per se*, but also to one or more of the golden lampstands of the future that Jesus is walking in the middle of as He dictates the letters.

In the first five letters, Jesus begins the letter by reiterating certain aspects of the first vision of the future (see chapter 1). It emphasizes the importance of the first vision and the need to keep it firmly in mind as the reader progresses through the Revelation. That is, the seven stars not only point with precision to the seven golden lampstands of the first vision, but also to all the other good things foretold in the many visions that follow. The importance of the first vision, and the star-messengers, cannot be overstated.

Jesus is actually reiterating, or clarifying, in the Ephesian letter that the seven Asian churches seen in His right hand in the vision are indeed to the right of Him. That is, Jesus is saying they are to the "right" of where He is now walking on the Isle of Patmos. That means Jesus is facing north, the orientation of all world maps. Of course, the early church did not possess such things as a compass, world maps or globes (not knowing the Earth is round until 1492); so it is safe to assume that much of the Revelation is not meant to be understood by the early Church but by later generations.

Nonetheless, while each letter may also be directed to one or more of the seven golden lampstands of the future, it is also apparent that the subject matter of each letter reflects the situation in the first century church to which it is addressed. The Ephesian church, for example, was the oldest of the churches in the Roman Province of Asia, and is appropriately mentioned first, and commended for its endurance (verses 2-3).

Ephesus was also a lampstand of the Church (but not a golden one). That is, Ephesus was the home of a bishop (or overseer) who oversaw all the other Asian churches, and not just the Christians within the city walls of Ephesus. Timothy was the first bishop, and when he left, John assumed the bishop duties for a time. (The seven golden lampstands are overseen by a "Patriarch" or "Pope," and not a "bishop").

In verse 2, Jesus tells the church of Ephesus—as He tells all seven churches—I know your works. Thus another theme of the Revelation is launched, i.e., an undeniable emphasis throughout for the need of good works. In chapter 20 we are told that in the final judgment, everyone will be judged according to their works. While critics say the Revelation places too much emphasis on works, it is consistent with the teachings of Jesus in the Gospels where (for example, in Matthew 16:27) He told His followers that He will reward each according to his or her works.

While the Revelation indeed confirms that each individual will be judged according to his or her works, in this verse Jesus is judging the works of an entire church. And it implies that not only will the Asian churches be judged according to their collective works, but Jesus is also signifying that He will similarly judge the seven golden lampstands of the future to which the messengers point.

The Ephesian church is the oldest of the seven Asian churches, founded by Paul on his second missionary journey, circa AD 49-52 (Acts 15:39-18:22), and Jesus commends the Ephesians twice for their endurance (in verses 2 & 3). Thus is introduced another theme of the Revelation—the love of Jesus for a Church that endures and works tirelessly and endlessly for His name's sake.

Also in verse 2, Jesus praises the Ephesian church for not tolerating evil, and for holding heresy trials, and finding guilty those who are not true apostles. After the fall of Jerusalem (in AD 70), the Ephesian Church grew in prominence and became one of the first churches other than Jerusalem to hold heresy trials. For this good work, the Ephesian church is commended (in verse 2 and again in verse 6).

Alas, after commending the Ephesians for their endurance, for their labor for His name's sake, and for holding heresy trials, Jesus then scolds them for forsaking their first love (verse 4) and their first works (verse 5). The Ephesian letter is intriguing because Jesus is critiquing the church where Paul, then Timothy and then John resided for a time. But we should also note that, according to Church historians, Timothy had left Ephesus years before, becoming the bishop of Thesalonica in his later years, and John had been in exile for about twelve years. Evidently, lacking a strong leader the caliber of Paul, Timothy or John, the Ephesian Church of the late first century was failing to do something they did at first.

One interpretation is that Jesus wants the Ephesians to simply return to doing works of love. The Greek word used here is *agape*, one of four words for love, meaning unqualified love, as when Jesus said, "No greater love has no man than this, that he lay down his life for his friends." Jesus tells us in the Gospels that all of the Law (of the Old Testament) can be summed up in two commandments. The first is "Love the Lord your God with all your heart, all your soul, and all your mind." The second is similar, "Love your neighbor as yourself" (Matthew 22:37-40). And Jesus adds a similar commandment in John's Gospel commanding His followers to "Love one another as I have loved you." (John 13:34). It may be that, by the end of the first century, the Ephesian Church had become too involved with heresy trials or whatever and was no longer displaying love for one another as they did at first.

But there is another scenario that fits at least as well, if not better. When kept in context with verse 3, it appears the Ephesian church may not have been exhibiting love for the name of Jesus or performing works in His name as it did at first. Moreover, the history books tend to bear that out.

The first recorded incidence of works of the Church being attributed to any name but Jesus occurred in Asia Minor less than two centuries later when St. Gregory the Wonderworker prayed to, and attributed wondrous works to, Mary the mother of Jesus. The Ephesian archbishopric grew phenomenally in the second and third centuries, but the words of Jesus suggest errors crept into the early Church through the Ephesian church, and early on.

Jesus appears to be saying to the Ephesian church at the cusp of the second century, return to the wondrous works of love attributed to His name, and not anyone else's name, including Mary's.

Not only in Asia, but all over the known world, the pagan masses came to be converted who had previously worshipped either the Greek Goddess Artemis or the Roman Goddess Diana. Moreover, following the example of Asia Minor, many of the thousands of new converts soon began to pray to, and to worship, the name of Mary more than the name of Jesus. In effect, it can be argued, Artemis and Diana were replaced by Mary.

In verse 5b, Jesus says the Ephesian lampstand will be removed from its place if they fail to repent.

The Fall of Ephesus

The Ephesian lampstand would indeed soon be removed from its place as signified in verse 5. By the middle of the fifth century, the Ephesian harbor began to silt up, and by the sixth century Ephesus became a ghost town.

While some may say it was a random act of God or providence, a little digging into the history books reveals that there may be more to it as Jesus suggests. The Ephesian letter deals with heresy trials (verses 2 and 6), so it behooves us to take a look at the calling of all the world's bishops to Ephesus in AD 43l, to examine the teachings of Nestorius concerning the name of Mary.

Ephesus was the appropriate setting because the name above the door of the Ephesian Church was "The Church of St. Mary" with no mention of Jesus. The Ephesians no doubt came to love Mary dearly because this was where she spent the last years of her life. Plus it can be surmised that not only was the Ephesian lampstand the first to pray to Mary, but it was likely the first Church to call her the Theotokos, or "Mother of God" in their prayers to her. By the fifth century, the practice had caught on in many other jurisdictions, but not all. Some bishops, led by Nestorius, objected and taught that it was wrong to call Mary the Theotokos—which can and does lead to Mary worship.

Debates soon raged throughout the kingdom, both in the Church and in the marketplace. So the Emperor, Theodosius II, called all the world's bishops to Ephesus to settle the matter. After much debate, the Ephesian Council ruled against Nestorius and decreed that there was nothing wrong with calling Mary "the Mother of God" or praying to her instead of Jesus.

It led to the first schism in the Church, which has to be very displeasing to Jesus because He often prayed for the Church to be united as one, as He and His Father are united as one. And any scientist will tell you, like Nestorius, that it is physically impossible for Mary to be the mother of God. That is, fifty percent of a child's genes are inherited from his or her mother, and fifty percent from his or her father. Therefore, Mary is technically the mother of the human-half of Jesus, not the God-half, despite what many theologians may say.

And almost immediately the Ephesus harbor began to silt up and the Ephesian lampstand was removed from its place—just as Jesus said it would be if the Ephesians continued worshipping His mother more than Him.

The Good News is, the current Patriarch of Constantinople is now holding talks with the Church of the East, i.e., the Nestorians, about coming back together in the restoration of all things.

In summary, the first Ecumenical Council (which condemned the Arian heresy) is one of the most highly praised events in the Bible (see Mat 24:31), but the other Councils (especially the one held in Ephesus), not so much (except maybe the second Ecumenical Council which also was about the Arian heresy). But after AD 381, errors began to creep into the Church. As Jesus tells us in the letter to Sardis, we are to keep the Gospel we have received from St. Peter and the early Church and not change it.

The Nicolaitans

In verse 6, Jesus returns to the subject of the Ephesians' good works, saying He is proud of the Ephesians for holding a heresy trial to examine the doctrine of the Nicolaitans, and not tolerating them. Very little is said about the Nicolaitans in this letter, but we meet them again in the letter to Pergamos where it is said their deeds of eating food sacrificed to idols and of committing sexual immorality are what is hated. These two transgressions are significant in that they are the two things strictly forbidden by the first council of the Church that was held in Jerusalem (see Acts 15). They are doubly significant in that Nicholas sat on that council—being one of the seven deacons of Jerusalem (see Acts 6:5). In the first commentary on the Revelation, Victorinus of Pettau said the followers of Nicholas devised at least two ceremonies—one to exorcise meat sacrificed to idols and another for those who had committed adultery—enabling them to be cleansed of their sin on the eighth day.

Other commentators say the Nicolaitans engaged in all sorts of pleasure, thinking all they had to do was believe, and through the grace of God, all their sins would be forgiven. Clement of Alexandria, for example, says that the Nicolaitans "abandon themselves to pleasure like goats … leading a life of self indulgence."

Peter was likely speaking of the Nicolaitans when he said, concerning Paul's teachings, "Our beloved brother Paul, according to the wisdom given to him, has written to you, as also in all his epistles, speaking in them of … things hard to understand, which those who are untaught and unstable twist to their own destruction" (II Peter 3:15-16—NKJV).

Peter addressed his epistles to the churches in the Roman provinces of Asia, Pontus, Galatia, Cappadocia and Bithnia (I Peter 1:1) which are all in western Asia Minor. So it can be seen from the epistles of Peter how quickly the Church in Asia Minor grew after Paul's three missionary journeys there and also how widely the teachings of Paul were twisted in the churches that were overseen by Ephesus.

It can well be argued that the admonitions of Jesus and Peter speak equally as well to the abuses of the doctrine of grace arising much later, especially in the West. Many sects of today twist the words of Paul by saying "once saved, always saved"—which tends to encourage Christians to sin all they want to without any fear of consequences, just as the Nicolaitans did.

The Spirit of the Letter

In verse 7, and at the end of each of the letters, a prophetic promise is made by "the Spirit" to the Churches, to the one that has an ear that hears or understands, and is "conquering." Because Spirit (or *Pneuma*) is capitalized in the Received Greek Text, the general consensus is that Jesus is referring to the Holy Spirit. But it may also be that the spirit of prophecy is meant, which is the ultimate proof of Jesus (see Rev 19:10).

To hear what the spirit (or Spirit) is saying to the Churches, it behooves us to look at the original Greek text. The first two words, *To Nikonti,* are best translated "To the one conquering" (and not the milder "the one overcoming" as many English Bibles mistranslate it). *Nikonti* is from the root word *nikao*, meaning to conquer and bring into subjection. In the first century, the Church was still small in numbers, had no weapons and no generals, and was not in a position to conquer. The change in speakers, as well as subject matter, signifies that the great promises of the seven Spirits are not being made to the seven Asian churches but to the Churches of the future to which they point.

The emphasis on conquering points to the turning point of history (October 27, AD 312) when the sign of the Son of man appeared in the clouds over Rome (fulfilling Matthew 24:30). In a dream that night St. Constantine again saw the sign, and Jesus appeared to him and said *"En touto nika"* or in English, "By this, conquer." From that day, the Church has been able to conquer, and Christianity remains the Earth's most dominant body-politic to this day, despite enduring great challenges. To the Church that conquers, a total of seven great promises are made.

The next phrase, *doso auto,* also presents a problem for English translators. It literally means "I will give to it, him, or her" depending on the context. Sometimes *auto* is not translated at all (which is grammatically OK in English), but when it is translated, it has typically been translated "to him" due to the lack in the English language of an all-inclusive third person singular pronoun. Thus, most English Bibles give the reader the impression that the seven promises are directed to individuals, and exclusively so. But the context makes it clear that "I will give to it" is the correct translation, meaning "I will give to the Church that conquers…"

So it is safe to say that the Church that conquers to the end will be granted to eat of the fruit and leaves of the tree of life in the middle of the paradise of God. That is, the seven great promises (at the end of the seven letters) are directed not to individuals but to lamp-stand assemblies, i.e., priests and kings, or Christian nations. The leaves of the tree of life are said to be for the healing of the twenty-four nations represented by their 24 fruits (see Rev 22:2).

In the beginning, the tree of life was present in the middle of the Garden of Eden, the first paradise of God, and later the tree of life is provided for us in the paradise of God of the future called the New Jerusalem. But there is much more to it than that. It can well be argued that here, Jesus is walking in the middle of an early version of the New Jerusalem. Doubters should note that the dimensions given for the New Jerusalem, about two million square miles in area, are the same as the square miles encompassed by the first Christian kingdom brought about by Constantine and the second coming of Jesus. Moreover, the Byzantine Empire endured for one thousand years as did the first Kingdom of God on Earth (i.e, ancient Israel). And soon—any day now—the final Kingdom of God will come to pass that is made up of twenty-four thrones that will rule the entire earth for a thousand years (see Rev 4:4 & 20:4). From the other letters, it can be deduced that one or more of the golden lampstands will conquer to the end and become the pillar(s) of the New Jerusalem. It follows then that the other lampstands will be removed from their place at some point. It can well be argued that most of the seven lampstands have indeed been removed from their place, beginning with Rome in AD 476.

For Further Study: The Many Falls of Rome

The Ephesian letter appears to prophetically signify that Jesus foreknew that ill fate would befall the Roman lampstand at the same moment in history when the Ephesian lampstand bit the dust.

Both events astounded the world. But the fall of Rome to the Lombards shook the world mightily. It can be assumed that Rome, like Ephesus, received its just reward. Either Rome was not exhibiting works of love as it did at first, or by the year AD 476 the Church in Rome failed to perform works of love in the name of Jesus as it did at first. If it appears to the reader that this commentary is now going off on a tangent, that's because it is (i.e., a tangent vector of the Ephesian messenger points to Rome).

The history books reveal that in Rome and throughout the Latin-speaking world, the Roman Goddess Diana was worshipped much like the Greek Goddess Artemis was worshipped in Ephesus and throughout the Greek-speaking world. Their names are virtually interchangeable, as in Acts 19:24, where Artemis is often translated as Dianna in western Bibles. So it came to pass in the fourth century, in the Roman Church, that after a mass conversion of the pagan masses, many of the former worshippers of the Roman Goddess Diana transferred their allegiance to Mary and began to attribute wondrous works to her name—as did former worshippers of Artemis in Asia Minor.

It is likely that several things contributed to Rome's disfavor with God and the early removal of the Roman lampstand from its place. For example, when the Roman Church gained great power in the fourth century, it began to burn at the stake all who disagreed in any small way with any of its many teachings, thereby not exemplifying love. Worse, by the middle of the fourth century, Rome also brought to trial and burnt at the stake all those who said it was wrong to call Mary the "ever virgin" mother of Jesus. That had to anger Jesus because the Bible clearly states Jesus had brothers and a sister (see Mark 6:3, Acts 15:13, Galatians 1:19), and it led to Mary-worship which Jesus very much dislikes. So the Roman lampstand immediately fell as did Ephesus, and at the same time.

To Rome's credit however, the Roman Church eventually converted the Lombards and the many other Barbarian tribes who invaded the western Roman Empire in the fourth and fifth centuries, and in time was able to partially restore the western lampstand in AD 800, albeit in Versailles, with the crowning of Charlemagne as the western Roman Emperor. With the decline of the French Kings in the mid tenth century, the western Roman Empire was revived under German Emperors and came to be known as the Holy Roman Empire.

Another fall of Rome, it can be argued, occurred in 1054 when the other golden lampstands excommunicated the Roman Church (for changing the Nicene Creed).

The Roman Church again declined in power in the sixteenth century due to the Reformation that rejected many suspect teachings of Rome including the dogma of the immaculate conception of Mary, the practice of attributing miracles to her, and the practice of calling her the "ever virgin" mother of Jesus.

Another fall of Rome's lampstand, it can argued, came in 1806 when Napoleon conquered both Rome and Germany and brought an end to the Holy Roman Empire.

Then in 1929 the Pope was removed from Rome and banished to the Vatican, the world's smallest nation.

In the latest development, there is now a group of Roman Catholics who are urging the Pope to make Mary a God equal to Jesus, the ultimate heresy. It does not bode well for the Roman Church.

And it may be that the Anglican Church, now the de facto head honcho of the West, will soon officially replace Rome as the western lampstand. That is, the Patriarch of Constantinople is now engaged in talks with the Archbishop of Canterbury with the stated goal of Canterbury joining with the Orthodox Churches in full communion, in effect replacing Rome's lampstand.

This commentary on the Roman Church should not be construed to mean that most Roman Catholics are not good Christians overall or that Roman Catholic nations will not be included in the twenty-four thrones that will soon rule the Earth for Jesus for a thousand years (see chapters 4 and 20).

The Fall of the Other Golden Lampstands

Following the fall of Rome (in 476), Jerusalem, Antioch and Alexandria fell to the Islamic hordes in AD 636-638. Part of the reason is that many Christians in those Churches had been convicted of embracing heresies and excommunicated, so Constantinople felt no obligation to come to their rescue. The Bulgarian and Serbian Patriarchates fell in the 14th century—except for Montenegro which was never defeated and has conquered to the end! In the next century, in 1453, Constantinople fell.

To Constantinople's credit, the Greek Church managed to stay in power for over a thousand years, and the Byzantine Empire can truly be called the golden years of the Church. There are doubtless many reasons for the fall of Constantinople, but one of the chief reasons for it is no doubt a very-nearly exclusive and full worship of Mary after the seventh ecumenical Council convened by Constantinople, which sided with the Roman Church in calling Mary an "ever-virgin." Shortly thereafter, the Greek cities in Asia Minor began to fall, one by one, to the Islamic hordes until Constantinople itself fell in 1453. The history books tell us that when Constantinople fell to the Islamic Turks, Constantinople's streets were full of people carrying icons of the virgin Mary and praying to her name. Nowhere is it recorded that even one of the millions of Christians in Constantinople on that fateful day prayed one word to the one name that could have saved them. In the Revelation and throughout the Bible, everything has a cause and effect even if it takes centuries to play out. There is no escaping the judgments of God.

The Serbian and Bulgarian Churches appear to be well on their way towards restoring their lampstands, and at least some Serbian churches no longer call Mary an "ever-virgin." That is probably one of the reasons God is blessing them (also see commentary on the fifth horseman of Rev 19).

And it may be that the Greek Church also will fully restore its lampstand by reconquering Constantinople in the coming restoration of all things. But the Greek Church will no doubt have to cease its worship of Mary (and praying to her instead of praying in the name of Jesus as Jesus tells us to do). It will no doubt take a miracle, but that is the business Jesus is in.

As for the Bulgarian Church, unfortunately I have never been to a Bulgarian Orthodox Church, so I have no idea what they teach concerning Mary. Therefore, I cannot shed light on that.

This commentary should not be construed to say that most Greek Orthodox Christians (and other Orthodox Christians) are not good Christian people, or that Greece will be excluded from the twenty-four thrones that will soon rule the Earth for Jesus for a thousand years.

Second Letter: A Literal Translation of Rev 2:8-11

> And to the messenger of the church in Smyrna write, These things says the First and the Last, who was dead, and came back to life: ⁹I know your works, tribulation, and poverty—but you are rich—and [I know] the blasphemy of those who say they are Jews and are not, but are a synagogue of Satan. ¹⁰Do not fear any of those things which you are about to suffer. Indeed, the devil is about to throw [some] of you into prison, that you may be tested, and you will have tribulation ten days. Be faithful until death, and I will give you the crown of life.
>
> ¹¹The one having an ear, let it hear what the Spirit says to the Churches: The one that conquers will not be hurt by the second death.

The Church in Smyrna

The messenger of the church in Smyrna is its coordinates which, in conjunction with the other coordinates, directs this letter to the seven golden lampstands of the future, as well as to Smyrna. The title Jesus takes, the First and the Last, is a name for God in the Old Testament, and it signifies that Jesus is also God, i.e., the Son of God. The fact that He died on the cross and then came back to life is offered as the ultimate proof.

Jesus knows the works of the Smyrna Church and their tribulation and poverty. The Smyrna church is one of the two Asian churches that Jesus finds no fault with, and they are still there today. But these days, in Smyrna, it is mainly NATO soldiers who worship in its ancient churches.

In John's day, many Christians experienced tribulation at the hands of Rome, and especially in Smyrna. And many Christians were poor, and especially in Smyrna, but Jesus says they are rich, meaning they will receive a rich reward in heaven.

In Smyrna there was a large population of Jews, and they held sway with the Roman authorities. And they did not like the Christians, mainly because the Church was taking away many Jews as converts. So they often made up blasphemous lies in order to get the Roman authorities to arrest them. Jesus says they are worshippers of Satan, not God.

As for the ten days of tribulation and imprisonment that Jesus predicts, there is much debate as to whether Jesus meant a literal ten days or ten years. That is, in many Bible prophecies, 1 day signifies 1 year. Some commentators think Jesus is referring to the imprisonment and execution of Polycarp, the Bishop of Smyrna, in AD 155. Historical sources do not say how long Polycarp was in prison awaiting his trial and sentencing; but justice was swift in those days, and ten days seems reasonable. Other commentators think Jesus is referring to an earlier persecution of Smyrna's Christians at the hands of emperor Trajan which lasted exactly ten years.

Jesus tells the Smyrna Christians to be faithful until death, and He will give them the crown of life, i.e., a glorious life after death in the New Jerusalem that awaits believers.

In verse 11, there is a change in speakers. The Spirit is talking to the seven golden lampstands of the future to which the messenger points. The Spirit says the Church that conquers will not be hurt by the second death. The term "second death" is not found anywhere else in the Bible (except the Revelation), and therefore, there is some debate as to what it means. But it most likely refers to the final white throne judgment that takes place after the Earth is destroyed by fire (see Revelation 20). Everyone is resurrected and judged according to their works, and those found worthy get to live on a new Earth in the New Jerusalem. All others are cast back into the fire (or what is left of the Earth) where they theoretically experience a second death. This verse, however, suggests that whole Churches are judged collectively and solely by whether or not they conquer to the end. That agrees with chapter 21 where it is said the tree(s) of life in the New Jerusalem are for the twenty-four Christian nations that conquer to the end.

Third Letter: A Literal Translation of Rev 2:12-17

And to the messenger of the church in Pergamos write, These things says the One having the sharp two-edged sword. [13]I know your works, and where you dwell, where the throne of Satan is. And you hold fast to My name, and did not deny My faith in the days in which Antipas My faithful witness was killed among you, where Satan dwells. [14]But I have a few things against you, because you have there some who hold the doctrine of Balaam, who taught Balak to throw a stumbling block before the sons of Israel, both to eat things sacrificed to idols and to commit fornication. [15]So have you also some holding the teaching of the Nicolaitans, which thing I hate. [16]Repent therefore, or else I will come to you quickly and I will make war with them with the sword of My mouth.

[17]The one having an ear let it hear what the Spirit says to the Churches. To the one that conquers I will give to [that one] of the hidden manna. And I will give to it a white gemstone, and on the gemstone a new name written which no one recognizes except the one receiving it.

The Church in Pergamos

The messenger of the church in Pergamos is its coordinates which, in conjunction with the other messengers, directs this letter to the seven golden lampstands of the future as well as to Pergamos. Connecting the seven great Patriarchal Churches of the future on a world map reveals the blade of a sharp two-edged sword, and Jesus, it truly can be said, is the one who wields it. The two-edged sword also represents the Word of God—and the words of Jesus—that cuts to the quick and leads to either eternal life or death (see Hebrews 4:12).

Jesus knows the works of the Pergamos church and mostly commends them. Pergamos is called the throne of Satan because it was the center of Caesar-worship in the Asian province. It is where there was a big temple honoring the godhead of Caesar. Because Christians refused to go along and say "Caesar is Lord," they were often imprisoned and sometimes executed. Yet the Pergamos Christians held fast and did not deny their faith in the Christian God even when Antipas was killed for his witness. (Nothing is known about Antipas today)

Even so, Jesus has a few things against them. We are told that some Pergamos Christians held the teaching of Balaam. Balaam brought down Israel by introducing corruption and idol worship, etc. into Israel by saying it was acceptable for the men to marry Moab women. Jesus is apparently saying some Pergamos Christians were married to non-Christians which is probably displeasing to Jesus, especially if it causes the Christian to sin. Jesus also hates the Nicolaitans who are discussed in detail in the commentary on the Ephesian letter.

In verse 16 Jesus tells the Pergamos church to repent, and reprimand and/or excommunicate the sinners, or else He will come himself and make war with them with the sword in His mouth. It is not real clear, but "them" probably refers to the sinners and not the whole church. The sword in the mouth of Jesus represents the Word of God

In verse 17 the Spirit is speaking to the seven golden lampstands of the future pointed to by the Pergamos messenger. To the one that conquers, two things are promised—hidden manna and a white gemstone with a new name written on it that no one recognizes. The term "hidden manna" harkens back to the Old Testament. In order for the Israelites to survive in the wilderness, God sent manna from heaven to sustain them (see Exodus 16). The white gemstone, assuming everything in the Revelation has two meanings, may refer back to one of the 12 gemstones worn by the high priest in the Holy of Holies (Exodus 28), but it also points to a gemstone that will be worn in the crown of one of the kings of the seven lamp-stand assemblies in the future.

The white gemstone with a new name written on it, that no one recognizes except for the one Church (and/or king) receiving it, points to a twentieth century event. It no doubt refers to the little pebble of a nation called Republica Srpska that no one on Earth recognizes except for the Serbian Church and king (or President). The implication is that, more so than any of the other golden lampstands, the Serbian Church has conquered to the end and will be rewarded both in heaven and in the glorious thousand year reign of the Church on earth about to take place. In the wilderness (defined as any non Judeo-Christian country), when the Serbs suffered for five hundred years under the rule of the Turks as prophesied by their prophets, God sustained them with "hidden manna" (not literally visible unless we assume it was hidden in the visible Eucharist bread), much like He did for the Israelites when they were in the wilderness (see Exodus 16). (For more on the Serbian Church, see commentary on Revelation 19).

Fourth Letter: A Literal Translation of Rev 2:18-28

And to the messenger of the church in Thyatira write, These things says the Son of God, the one having eyes like a flame of fire, and feet like burnished metal. [19]I know your works, love, service, faith, and your patience; and as for your works, the last are more than the first. [20]But I have a few things against you, because you allow the wife, your Jezebel, who calls herself a prophetess, to teach and seduce My servants to commit fornication and eat things sacrificed to idols. [21]And I gave her time to repent of her fornication, and she did not repent. [22]Behold, I am throwing her into a sickbed, and those who commit adultery with her into great tribulation, unless they repent of their deeds. [23]I will kill her children with death, and all the churches shall know that I am He who searches the minds and hearts. And I will give to each one of you according to your works.

[24]Now I say to you, the rest in Thyatira, as many as do not have this doctrine, who have not known the depths of Satan as they say, I am not putting on you any other burden. [25]But hold fast what you have till I come. [26]And to the one conquering and keeping My works until the end, I will give authority over the nations—

[27]He [or that one] shall shepherd them with a rod of iron;

Like clay vessels, they shall be smashed—

as I also have received from My Father. [28] And I will give to it the Morning Star. [29] The one having an ear, let it hear what the Spirit says to the Churches.

The Church in Thyatira

The messenger of the Church in Thyatira is its coordinates which, in conjunction with the other messengers, forward the letter on to the seven golden lampstands of the future. But most of it is about Thyatira.

Jesus introduces Himself as the One having eyes like flames of fire and feet like burnished metal—His "transfigured" (or supernatural) body in which He appears in the Revelation. He says He knows the good works of the Thyatira church—their love, ministry, faith, their patience, and their works—the last being more than the first, which is good.

But Jesus has a few things against them—because they allowed a false prophetess to seduce members of the Church into committing fornication and to eat things sacrificed to idols. As for the identity of Jezebel, historians tell us nothing of a Christian prophetess in Thyatira, but they do say Thyatira was quite famous for its prophetesses. We do know that, like the Jezebel of old, she was someone's wife, and she taught and seduced God's servants to commit fornication and eat things sacrificed to idols—the very two things forbidden by the first Church Council, held in Jerusalem as recorded in Acts. It is not clear if Jesus is referring to literal fornication or, as often in the Bible, the sin of embracing a false God or false doctrine.

In any case, Jesus says he will wait no more for her to repent, and He will cast her into a sickbed, and He will also kill her children. And the ones committing fornication with her will also experience great tribulation unless they repent. Killing her children seems extremely harsh for a God of love, but God's love is a very tough love. In the Old Testament, God sometimes punishes people to the tenth generation.

But Jesus will not punish the whole Church. He knows each person's mind and heart, and He will give to each one according to their works.

The prophetic promise of the Spirit in this letter, like the promise at the end of the Pergamos letter, points to the Serbian Church. That is, the Serbs, like no other Christian Church on Earth, have conquered to the end and can truly be said to rule with a rod of iron—as evidenced by the Srebronica Massacre that resulted in thousands of bodies for the birds of the air to feast on. The promise of the Spirit seems to be signifying that the Serbs will be given authority over the nations for the next one thousand years and will annihilate them like smashing a clay pot if they rebel. Jesus says He will pass on the Morning Star to the golden lampstand that conquers to the end. In Revelation 22, Jesus tells us that He is the Bright Morning Star, also called the Star of David. It represents a powerful Jew from the line of David who will rule the Earth with a rod of iron. Here Jesus is saying He will transfer that power to the golden lampstand that conquers to the end.

For Further Study: When is "the end"?

This letter begs the question, "When is the end?" In recent years there have been many thousands of wild predictions made by futurists as to when the end will come. And they are the main reason the world laughs at Christians because none of their wild predictions have come true. This commentary will uphold the traditional view—or at least the traditional view among Dispensationalists—that the "end" is marked by the end of the thousand year Day Six of Genesis 1—known as the Day of Man—and the beginning of Day Seven, called The Day of the Lord and alternately, in the Revelation, That Great Day of God Almighty.

The end of Day Six and the beginning of Day Seven can be computed two ways—either on the sacred 360-day Hebrew calendar used in Old Testament prophesies, or using the Christian calendar in use today.

On the 360-day Hebrew calendar, the end of Day Six and the beginning of Day Seven was on the seventh day of the Six-Day War. One day, when I took my mother to get a free meal for the elderly, we were seated next to an elderly Jewish man. He said he had fought in the Six-Day War, and on the seventh day, he and a few other soldiers decided to go sight-seeing in the new territory they had just conquered. They went into the Church of the Nativity and took a picture of the six-pointed star marking the spot where Jesus was born. (It was made into a fourteen-pointed star by the Roman Catholic Crusaders who did not like six-pointed stars, but you can still see faint traces of the Star of David). He said when they had the picture developed a few days later, there was Jesus standing in the middle of the six-pointed star. And he said the Jewish authorities, when they heard about it, were not amused and erected a big sign saying "No Cameras Allowed" that remains to this day.

On the other hand, the Revelation indicates, or signifies, that 2001, the beginning of the third millennium AD on the calendar in use today, is the beginning of the Day of the Lord. That is, just as I and perhaps a few other dispensationalists predicted, "The Battle of That Great Day of God Almighty"—also known as the Battle of Ar Mageddon—began in 2001 right on time, on 9/11, when also the Euphrates was dry. The Good News is that it is the final battle between good and evil, and it will result in the latest face of the seventh head of Satan being so soundly defeated by 24 Christian nations that Satan will not be heard from again for a thousand years.

In short, the end is here, and the Holy Land has been given to the Jews, and the rest of the earth has been (or soon will be) given to Christians, a branch of the Jews, just as prophesied over 3000 years ago in Genesis.

The Orthodox View of the End

It would not be right to end this discussion of the end without also giving the reader the more official Orthodox view of the end, which sums things up beautifully.

From *"Ultimate Things"* by Dennis Engleman, page 1:

> The modern age has ended. Today many things indicate that we are going through a transitional period, when it seems that something is on the way out and something else is painfully being born. It is as if something were crumbling, decaying, and exhausting itself, while something else, still indistinct, were arising from the rubble. [a quote of Vaclav Havel]

> History has been fulfilled, and what will follow is beyond the limits of prior human experience. We stand at the end of the modern world and the beginning of whatever we will eventually call this new world that is coming to be. [a quote of James Davidson]

So there you have it. It is the view of many eschatologists around the world that the modern age has ended, and we are in the infancy of something new.

Fifth Letter: A Literal Translation of Revelation 3:1-6

> And to the messenger of the church in Sardis write: These things says the One having the seven Spirits of God and the seven star. I know your works, and that you have a name that you are alive, but you are dead. [2]Be watching, and keep the remaining things which you are about to throw away, for I have not found your works to be completed before God. [3]Remember therefore what you have received and heard, and hold fast and repent. If you do not watch, I will come upon you like a thief, and you will not know what hour I will come upon you.

> [4]But you have a few names in Sardis who have not defiled their garments, and they shall walk with me in white because they are worthy.

> [5]The one conquering, this one will be arrayed in white garments, and by no means will I blot out his name from the Book of Life, and I will confess his name before my Father, and before His angels. [6]The one having an ear, let it hear what the Spirit says to the Churches.

The Church in Sardis

As in the previous letters, Jesus begins by reminding the reader of important aspects of the all-important first vision of the Revelation, which is the key to understanding the rest of the otherwise very mysterious Revelation of the future. The seven stars and the seven Spirits are arguably the most important. The seven stars serve as seven star-like messengers that very accurately point the reader to the seven golden lampstands that the seven Spirits of God are to sit on and give light to the seven parts of the earth. The seven stars also guide the reader to all of the other good things foretold in the Revelation.

This is a very short letter, and the only two things Jesus says about the Sardis church is that they have a name (or reputation) for being alive, but are dead, and they need to remember the Gospel they have received, and keep it and not change it. It is hard to know exactly what Jesus means by that, but today when we say a Church is dying, it typically means the church is losing members. To stay alive and grow, a church indeed needs to constantly attract new members, but it all starts with sharing and living the Gospel we have received, which is what Jesus is urging the Sardis Church, and all Churches to do.

Some in Sardis have not defiled their white garments, which represent good works, and they will walk with Jesus in white because they are deemed worthy.

The promise of the Spirit in this letter, more so than in the other letters, can be deemed to apply to individuals as well as to a whole Church. The Greek word for conquer means military conquest, which takes an army, but the promise, it can be argued, also applies to individual soldiers as well as to the Church that conquers. In other words, the Spirit appears to be saying every Christian soldier in every Christian nation has a guaranteed place in heaven.

This letter, and especially the words of the Spirit, is directed, through vectors, to the seven golden lampstands of the Church primarily, but also to the Anglican and Episcopalian Churches (which can be considered to be an eighth golden lampstand which God causes to spring up after the Roman lampstand is excommunicated). The Spirit is especially talking about the one that conquers for hundreds and thousands of years and does not change the Gospel one iota from the way it was received from St. Peter and the early Church.

On a personal note, I'm afraid that my Church, the Episcopal Church, has soiled its garment by drastically changing things in the ordination of gay priests and bishops, and in the approval of, and the performing of, same-sex marriages. And now the Episcopal Church has lost a lot of members and is dying (just like the Sardis church). All of the letters are so prophetic and so true.

For Further Study

Is any Church still doing & saying everything as it was done by St. Peter & the early Church?

Amazingly, Yes, and that Church could be seen in Houston until recently.

On a personal note, I have been disgruntled for quite some time with the way my Church, the Episcopal Church, keeps changing things. So, about 20 years ago, I decided I would search for a Church that still does and says everything exactly as it was done in the first century, and I planned to join that Church if I could find such a church. The Revelation says it does exist, so I had some hope that I could find one in my neck of the woods.

And Lo and behold, I found it. It is the Serbian Orthodox Church in Houston, Texas. But not the Serbian Orthodox Church in nearby Galveston, which has been there for approximately one hundred twenty years and in some ways is very Americanized compared to the Houston version of the same Church. The Serbs in Houston are fresh off the boat from Serbia, and still do things the old way.

Although I managed to do just about everything wrong from the moment I walked in (and sat on the left side with the women), I was quite impressed when I found the Serbian Church in Houston, and I asked the priest what it would take for me to join his Church. He said the first thing I would have to do is say I give up all my beliefs. And I said it took me sixty years to arrive at my beliefs, and I was not prepared to give any of them up—to which he replied I could not join his Church and I was very saddened. But that was just the first hurdle I would have to go through. The second is, I would also have to bow with my head all the way to the ground the way the Serbs do (and the early Church did) at several times during Holy Communion. And they do not throw down a pad first like Muslims do. All the Serbs seem to be able to do it with little effort; but at my age, and being an out-of-shape Episcopalian, it is somewhat difficult for me to do and I gained a new appreciation for the Episcopalian well-padded kneelers. To make a long story short, I have now returned to the Episcopal Church, and for several reasons. For one thing, I speak English, not Serbian (or Slavic), and I suspect God wants me to stay in the English-speaking Church that I was born into. Plus, the Serbian church is on the other side of Houston (approximately fifty miles), and I am not keen on the idea of contributing to global warming when there is an Episcopal church a few blocks from me that I can walk to if the weather is pretty.

Yet I am sure, from the Sardis letter and many other verses in the Revelation, that Jesus (and God) is very pleased with the Serbs and will someday cause them to surpass the United States Church as the most powerful nation on Earth, and they will lead twenty-four Christian nations in a glorious thousand year reign of the Church.

But the Serbian Church (in Houston) no longer bows like that, and it would not be right to end this Further Study without also mentioning the Antioch Orthodox Church in Houston. It is made up of about half Arab Christians (mostly from Lebanon) and the other half mostly disgruntled Episcopalians such as me—based on what I have read on the Internet regarding the Antiochian Church and from my observation of the Houston congregation. There, about half of the men (mostly the Arab half) stood in the aisles and bowed with their head all the way to the floor at the appropriate times, and all the women sat in the pews where they had padded kneelers identical to the Episcopal Church. Any of the men could sit with their wife or a female friend if they wanted (unlike in the Serbian Church). I thought it was an excellent blending of two very different cultures and of the more important old ways with a little modern convenience. I do not know for sure what Jesus thinks about that, but Lebanon has conquered to the end despite being in the heart of the Middle East powder keg, and that is definitely pleasing to Jesus. Ultimately, in the restoration of all things to come, the Antiochian Church may even be able to retake Antioch. And that would greatly please Jesus.

The Serbian and Antiochian Churches also say everything just like the early Church did (as far as I can tell). For example, at the point of the Eucharist where the Greek Orthodox Church and the Roman Church say "the ever-virgin Mary," I heard the Serbian and Antiochian priests say "the virgin Mary," which I am sure also pleases Jesus (see commentary on the letter to Ephesus).

Sixth Letter: A Literal Translation of Revelation 3:7-13

And to the messenger of the church in Philadelphia write, These things says the Holy One, who is true, the One having the key of David, the One who opens and no one shuts, and shuts and no one opens: [8]I know your works. Behold, I have set before you an open door, and no one can shut it; for you have a little strength, have kept My word, and have not denied My name. [9]Behold, I am giving those of the synagogue of Satan, who say they are Jews and are not, but are lying—behold, I will make them come and worship before your feet, and they shall know that I have loved you. [10]Because you have kept My command to endure, I also will keep you from the hour of trial which shall come upon the whole world, to test those who dwell on the earth. [11]Behold, I am coming quickl y! Hold fast what you have so that no one may take your crown.

[12]The one that conquers I will make a pillar in the temple of My God, and [that Church] shall by no means go out any more. I will write on it the name of My God and the name of the city of My God, the New Jerusalem, which comes down out of heaven from My God. And I will write on it My new name. [13]The one having an ear, let it hear what the Spirit says to the Churches.

The Church in Philadelphia

To the messenger of the church in Philadelphia, Jesus introduces himself as "The One who is holy, the One who is true..." In the Old Testament, and until the Revelation, God the Father is the only one called "the One who is holy." Here, Jesus is saying that He and the Father are united as One, the Holy One. "The One who is true," like many things in the Revelation, can be said to have two meanings. One meaning appears to be that Jesus is very real and is standing right in front of John. A second meaning is that every word of Jesus is true and/or will come true because He does not lie.

"The One who has the key of David, the One who opens and no one shuts, and shuts and no one opens" is a quote of Isaiah 22:22. Jesus is that One, and it can refer to most everything, but it especially has meaning for the Philadelphia church. That church, which Jesus could find no fault with, is still there today.[1] Jesus has set before the Philadelphia church an open door that no one can shut because they have a little strength, have kept His word, and have not denied His name.

As in Pergamos, some Jews were causing some trouble in Philadelphia. Jesus calls them the synagogue of Satan and says that, at His second coming, He will cause them to worship at the feet of the Philadelphia Christians. That happened in AD 312, when the sign of Christ appeared in the clouds, and Jesus appeared to Constantine and said, "By this conquer." That is just the opposite of what most Jews think. They think they will someday rule the world based on several Old Testament prophecies, but a careful reading reveals that a branch of the Jews will rule the Earth. That branch is Christianity.

Because the Philadelphia church has kept the command of Jesus to endure, Jesus will keep them from "the hour of trial, the one about to come upon the whole world to test those who dwell on the Earth." It is not clear what hour of trial Jesus has in mind here, but it is most probably the "hour of trial" dished out by either the sixth head or the seventh head of the Satanic beast of the Revelation—the sixth head being pagan Rome, the seventh head being the Islamic hordes that overran Asia Minor several centuries later. In both cases, unlike the other Asian churches, the Philadelphia church escaped pretty much unscathed.

In verse 11 and throughout the Revelation, Jesus says He is coming quickly. And the history books say He did indeed return quickly, in AD 312. Yet there are many thousands of Christians who, for some reason, try to construe that to mean He will return in our future, some two thousand years later.

The promise of the Spirit to the one that conquers both reflects the conquering ability of the Philadelphia church, and, through its messenger, is also directed to the golden lampstands it points to that have conquered to the end.

The Philadelphia church definitely knew (knows) all about name changes. As everyone probably knows, Philadelphia means City of Brotherly Love. It was founded around BC 150 and was named after the brotherly love of Attalus for his brother Eumenes. Then in AD 17, an earthquake devastated Philadelphia and ten other Asian cities. The emperor Tiberius was generous and rebuilt Philadelphia.

In gratitude, Philadelphia changed its name to Neocaesaria, or "New City of Caesar." Later, in the days of emperor Vespasian, Philadelphia was in gratitude to change its name again, to Flavia; for Flavus was the family name of the emperor. Neither of the new names lasted, and in time the name Philadelphia returned. In very recent years, the name was changed again, this time to Alasehir which means "City of God."

The golden lampstand that conquers to the end will be made a pillar in the temple of God and shall by no means go out any more. Jesus says He will write on it several names: the name of God; and the name of the City of God, the New Jerusalem, that comes down from heaven from God; plus the new name of Jesus. That seems like a lot of names, but it may be that Jesus is talking about one name that conveys all of those meanings.

1. Source: *"The Revelation of John, Vol. 1"* by William Barclay, P.160. Westminster Press, 1960

Seventh Letter: A Literal Translation of Revelation 3:14-22

And to the messenger of the church in Laodicea write, These things says the Amen, the Faithful and True Witness, the Beginning of the creation of God, [15]I know your works, that you are neither cold nor hot. I wish you were cold or hot. [16]So then, because you are lukewarm, and neither cold nor hot, I will vomit you out of My mouth. [17]Because you say, I am wealthy and I have become rich, and I have need of nothing, and do not know that you are the wretched one, the pitiable one, and poor, blind, and naked, [18]I counsel you to buy from Me gold refined by fire, so that you may become rich; and white garments, that you may be clothed, and the shame of your nakedness may not appear; and eye salve, so that you may anoint your eyes in order that you may see.

[19]As many as I love, I rebuke and I chasten. Be zealous therefore and repent. [20]Behold, I stand at the door and I am knocking. If anyone hears My voice and opens the door, then I will come in to him and I will dine with him, and he with Me.

[21]To the one that conquers, I will grant to sit with Me in My throne, as I also conquered and sat down with My Father in His throne. [22]The one having an ear, let it hear what the Spirit says to the Churches.

The Church in Laodicea

On a personal note, up to this point, this commentary has mainly been critiquing other Churches when the words of Jesus pointed to it. But now, in an effort to be completely fair and balanced, I will here critique my own Church which is definitely pointed to, both subject-wise and vector-wise. That is, the Laodicea messenger is the source of three vectors that point to the three divisions of the western Patriarchate. One vector points to New York City, the headquarters of the Episcopal Church, and the other two vectors point to Canterbury and Rome. Extending the first vector a little bit further, it points to the US national church, i.e., the National Cathedral in Washington DC where virtually all of our presidents have worshipped.

Extending the vector still further, it points to the mother church of another nation, where I happen to reside (called Texas). On most Sundays the worshippers were Episcopalians, but if Santa Anna came around they were Roman Catholics (else they would all be shot). It is also worth noting that the rector was called the Elder (or Presbyter), and not "Father" as most Episcopals call their rector today (which is not pleasing to Jesus—see Mat 23:9). (For lack of a better term, my view could be called "Texas old-school").

Jesus is the Amen who witnesses everything in the last days just as He did in Asia Minor in the late first century. He is the beginning of the creation of God, or as Jesus says in the Gospels, He is the cornerstone that the builders rejected.

The Episcopal and Anglican Churches, and Rome for that matter, may be good at conquering, but they can all be said to be pretty rich and somewhat "lukewarm" spiritually. Jesus suggests that the western Churches are in danger of being vomited out of His mouth because we in the West tend to say, "I am wealthy and I have become rich and have need of nothing."

This letter can be hypothesized to apply, by way of many tangent vectors, to all rich Christians everywhere, especially those who do not buy gold in heaven by helping to feed, clothe, and house the needy Christians they see around them every day. Jesus is always hard on rich people. In the Gospels, Jesus said "It is easier for a camel to go through the eye of a needle than for a rich man to enter heaven." But He didn't say it was impossible. There are some billionaires (Warren Buffet and Bill Gates for example) who have given away about 99 percent of their wealth, and I suspect that maybe, just maybe, St. Peter will let them in. But they will have to give up their agnosticism and join an established Church (established by St. Peter and his successors, both kings and archbishops) otherwise Peter probably isn't going to let them in.

This letter especially points to the Episcopal Church which, more so than any other Church, is known as the Church of the rich and powerful. Jesus appears to be saying to the Episcopalians mainly, but also other rich Christians, to buy eye salve (from Him) and open their eyes to the error of their ways, and buy a white garment to hide their nakedness. (The white garment represents good works).

One thing Jesus tells all the Churches to do (in the Sardis letter) is to keep the Gospel they have received, and not change it every time the wind blows in order to try to conform to the world, and to be "politically correct." That means that one thing Jesus is very likely displeased with, regarding the Episcopal Church, is the ordination of gay priests and bishops and the performing of same-sex marriages. While it is true that most gays are born with the "gay" gene, the Bible tells us we are all born with the tendency to sin in one way or another. And it says when we act on it, we are in grave danger of hell fire unless we repent. It can well be argued that same-sex marriages, more than anything else on Earth, are an abomination to God (see Leviticus 20:13). Jesus is standing at the door knocking, asking Episcopalians (especially the presiding bishop) to repent, as also on numerous occasions the Anglican Church has asked the presiding bishop to do, but to no avail.

But one thing that Jesus has to be proud of the Episcopal Church for is L4L (Love for the Least) that many Episcopalians contribute to. It is a multi-denominational charity headed by Jerry Kramer (originally from the church that I attend). They have brought food and water to the neediest of the needy around the world, while also saving their souls. And the one thing Jesus is probably the most happy about, is that L4L has recently opened a mission in northern Iraq, in the epicenter of the Battle of That Great Day Almighty, otherwise known as Ar Mageddon. And L4L, unlike Obama, et al, is caring for 2 million refugees there, and not bringing them here. And L4L is building free housing, but only for Christian families (unlike Obama). Also, as far as I know, L4L is the first international organization to recognize the new nation of Kurdistan now being born (which is fast becoming a Christian nation and fulfilling many prophecies).

So I hold out some hope that Jesus will not spit my church out of His mouth.

In the Laodicea letter, Jesus is urging all lukewarm Christians, and/or Churches, to repent and to conquer to the end, and then they will be granted to sit with Jesus in His throne. Jesus (or the Spirit) is looking ahead to the prophecy in the next chapter, and later expanded on in chapter 20, that twenty-four thrones will rule the earth with Jesus for a glorious one thousand years. (And all the signs point to a new world order comprised of 24 Christian nations coming to pass in 2017—see "2017 in Bible Prophecy" on last page).

This commentary should not be construed to mean that all Episcopal/Anglican/Roman-Catholic Churches are lukewarm, or that all rich Christians are failing to do good works, or that the US, the UK, or Catholic nations won't be included in the twenty-four Christian nations that will soon rule the Earth with Jesus in a glorious millennial reign of the Church.

PART 2
The Second Vision

A Literal Translation of Revelation 4

After these things I saw, and behold, a door opened in the sky, and the first voice which I heard was like a trumpet speaking with me, saying, Come up here, and I will show you things which must occur after these things. [2]Immediately I came to be in [the] spirit, and behold, a throne was set in the sky, and on the throne was One sitting [3]similar in appearance to jasper and sardius stones, and there was a rainbow around the throne similar in appearance to emeralds.

[4]And around the throne were twenty-four thrones, and on the thrones were sitting twenty-four elders clothed in white garments, and they had crowns of gold on the their heads. [5]And from the throne proceeded lightnings, and voices and thunders, and seven lamps of fire were burning before the throne, which are seven Spirits of God.

[6]And before the throne was something like a sea of glass similar to crystal, and in the midst of the throne and round the throne were four living creatures, full of eyes before and behind. [7]And the first living creature was like a lion, and the second living creature was like a calf, and the third living creature had a face like a man, and the fourth one was like a flying eagle.

[8]And each of the four living creatures had six wings, around and within full of eyes, and they never cease by day and by night, saying, Holy, holy, holy, Lord God Almighty, who was, and who is, and who is coming. [9]And whenever the living creatures give glory and honor and thanks to the One sitting on the throne, to the One living to the ages of the ages, [10]the twenty-four elders fall down before the One sitting on the throne and worship the One living to the ages of the ages, and cast their crowns before the throne, saying, [11]Worthy are You, our Lord and God, the

Holy One, to receive the glory, and the honor, and the power, because You created all things, and by your will they exist and were created.

The 4 living creatures and 24 elders, by Pat Marvenko Smith

Things Prophesied

This vision, that John sees in the sky, is not meant (primarily) to be a vision of heaven—despite what many Christians seem to assume—but is said to be a vision of "things which must occur after these things."

The vision reflects, or signifies, the situation we have on Earth today. In 2017, a twenty-fourth Christian nation is expected to be added to NATO which is the de facto ruler of the Earth. The twenty-four Christian nations are represented by the twenty-four elders surrounding the throne of God. A little research into the history of the twenty-four Christian nations reveals they can all trace their roots back to four Churches descended from the first century Church, and represented here by the four living creatures.

The four living creatures are said to have six wings covered front and back with eyes. The eyes represent the tens of thousands of individual congregations that make up each of the four Churches. They are the eyes through which we see God, and through which He sees us. The four Churches, it can truly be said, continually sing "Holy, Holy, Holy, Lord God Almighty" (followed by "God in Three Persons, Blessed Trinity"). They are the Orthodox Church, the Roman Catholic Church, the Anglican Church, and the Episcopal Church. (For more on the four living creatures, see commentary on the four horsemen of chapter 6).

The seven lamps of fire in front of the throne are said to represent seven Spirits of God. Tying this vision together with the first vision, they are quite obviously the lamps that are to sit atop the seven golden lampstands and give light to the seven parts of the Earth. That is, they represent the seven Patriarchates of the Church that oversee the earth, and bring the light of the Gospel to its seven parts.

The twenty-four Christian thrones (or nations) will soon rule the Earth for Jesus in a glorious thousand year reign of the Church (see chapter 20). They will bring glory and honor to God, the One who created them and everything that exists.

A Literal Translation of Revelation 5 (Second Vision, cont'd)

And I saw in the right hand of the One sitting on the throne a scroll, having been written inside and outside and having been sealed with seven seals. ²And I saw a strong angel proclaiming with a loud voice, Who is worthy to open the scroll and to loose its seals?

³And no one was able in the heaven above, nor on the earth, nor underneath the earth, to open the scroll, nor to look at it. ⁴And I was weeping much, because no one was found worthy to open the scroll nor to look at it.

⁵And one of the elders said to me, Do not weep. Behold the lion out of the tribe of Judah, the root of David, has prevailed to open the scroll, and to loose its seven seals. ⁶And I saw, and behold, in the midst of the throne, and of the four living creatures, and in the midst of the elders, a Lamb stood as it had been slain, having seven horns and seven eyes, which are the seven Spirits of God, which are sent to all [or the seven parts of] the earth, ⁷And He came and took the scroll out of the right hand of the One sitting on the throne.

⁸And when he took the scroll, the four living creatures and the twenty-four elders fell down before the Lamb, each having a harp and golden bowls full of incense, which are the prayers of the saints. ⁹And they sing a new song, saying, You are worthy to take the scroll and to open its seals, because you were slain, and You redeemed us to God by your blood out of every tribe and tongue and people and nation, ¹⁰and You have made us kings and priests to our God, and we will reign on the earth.

¹¹And I looked, and I heard the voice of many angels around the throne and the living creatures and the elders—and the number of them was myriads of myriads and thousands of thousands—¹²saying with a loud voice, Worthy is the Lamb who was slain to receive the power, and the wealth and wisdom and strength and honor and glory and blessing!

¹³And every creature which is in heaven and on the earth and under the earth and on the sea and all things in them, I heard saying, To the One sitting on the throne, and to the Lamb, be the blessing, and the honor, and the glory and the power to the ages of the ages. Amen. ¹⁴And the four living creatures said Amen! And the twenty-four elders fell down and worshipped the One living to the ages of the ages.

Things Prophesied

The main thing to take away from this chapter is that the Revelation can only be opened by the coming of Jesus, the Lamb of God. The history books tell us that happened in AD 312, on October 27th, when the sign of Christ appeared in the clouds, and Jesus appeared to St. Constantine and said, "By this, conquer." And that is what Constantine promptly did, riding a white horse and carrying a bow. Ever since that day, Christian nations have been the dominant force on Earth, and we will rule the Earth to the end (see Matthew 24:30 and Revelation 6:1-2).

We should also note that here, in this symbolic picture of Jesus, He has seven horns and seven eyes, which are said to be seven Spirits of God sent out to the seven parts of the Earth. We can assume that the eyes are in, or closely associated with, the horns. Like the lamp and stand, it illustrates the relationship between Church and State. The Church (or the seven eyes) attends to spiritual matters, and the king (or horn) attends to defending the Church and to conquering. The seven Church and State assemblies (or lamp-stand assemblies) that soon came to be established in the seven parts of the Earth (beginning in AD 325) are a direct result of the second coming of Jesus.

PART 3
Opening of the Seven Seals

The First Horseman: A Literal Translation of Revelation 6:1-2

And I saw when the Lamb opened one of the seals; and I heard one of the four living creatures saying with a voice like thunder, Come and see. ²And I looked, and behold, a white horse. He who sat on it had a bow; and a crown was given to him, and he went out conquering and to conquer.

Things Prophesied

In Revelation 5, we are told that the Revelation can only be opened by the coming of Jesus, the Lamb of God. The history books tell us that the second coming was in AD 312, when the sign of Christ appeared in the clouds, i.e., a chi-rho, and Jesus appeared to St. Constantine and said, "By this, conquer." And that is what Constantine promptly did. First, he put the sign on his labarum and on all of his army's armor. Then he mounted his white horse, and carrying a bow, he conquered Rome and all the known world for Jesus.

There will probably be some Christians who say, "But there was no rapture." Instead of Paul's "rapture", Constantine sent his messengers with a trumpet and gathered the elect of all the Church together, to Nicea, just as prophesied by Jesus in Matthew 24:31. All attendees said they felt as though they were in heaven.

The history books say that the appearance of the sign of Christ in the clouds on October 27, AD 312, marks the turning point of history because ever since that day, Christian nations have been the dominant force on Earth. That is what Jesus came to do—to rule the Earth through His followers. (In Luke 19:27, Jesus makes it clear that He does not kill anyone upon returning with a kingdom, and His followers are to do the killing of all His enemies).

We should note that the first horseman is introduced by the first of the four living creatures that are first seen in chapter 4. They represent the four Churches that have given us the four Christian superpowers (or horsemen) that have ruled the Earth for the last seventeen hundred years. The first one, the lion, represents either the Orthodox Church or, more likely, the entire Church when all the Church was united as one. That allowed the early Church to roar like a lion for a while—until most of the Antioch Church and the Alexandria Church split off in the 5th and 6th centuries, and were subsequently conquered by the seventh head of Satan (i.e, the Islamic hordes).

That is a traditional historicist view of the first horseman.[1]

Constantinople is pointed to by the star guide of Revelation 1 which guides the reader to all of the good things foretold.

1. At least one of the over 100 editions of the Geneva Bible (carried by the Puritans on the Mayflower) has a running commentary on the Revelation in the margins which says Constantine was the first horseman. This commentary is intended as an update of the 16th century historicist view, showing all of the things that have been fulfilled since then.

For Further Study: When did Constantine become a Christian?

There will probably be some who say Constantine was not a Christian or that he did not become a Christian until he was on his deathbed. But the Greek Orthodox Church says he converted and became a Christian that day when he saw the sign of Christ in the clouds and again in a dream a bit later (when Jesus appeared to him). At that point he became what the Greek Church calls "a Christian in training" when translated into English. It is true that he was not baptized until much later, but it was not because he did not want to be. He had to graduate from training class first.

The Second Horseman: A Literal Translation of Revelation 6:3-4

> And when He opened the second seal, I heard the second living creature saying, Come and see. 4And another horse, fiery red, went out. And it was granted to the one who sat on it to take peace from the earth, and that they may kill each other; and there was given to him a great sword.

Things Prophesied

The five horsemen of the Revelation can be thought of as five dispensations of the second coming. Following the Byzantine Empire, the second horseman to rule the Earth for Jesus was Roman Catholic kings who conquered with a great sword, and took peace from the Earth with their Crusades—when they did manage to kill some enemies of Jesus in the Holy Land as intended, but they also tended to kill everyone in sight, including Jews and even other Christians. It can truly be said that they took peace from the earth.

The kings and knights of the Middle Ages generally rode stout red (or chestnut-colored) horses with Arabian blood that are better able than white horses to support the added weight of the knight's heavy armor. Plus, the stouter Arabian horses added some extra force behind the thrust of their great swords (or lances).

The living creature that introduces the second horseman is the calf, which obviously represents the Roman Catholic Church because it gave us the Roman Catholic kings, but it is not very flattering. A calf has virtually no prowess or conquering abilities.

The Pope and many of the capitals of the Roman Catholic kings are pointed to by the star guide of Revelation 1.

The Third Horseman: A Literal Translation of Revelation 6:5-6

> And when He opened the third seal, I heard the third living creature say, Come and see. So I looked, and behold, a black horse, and he who sat on it had a pair of scales in his hand. [6]And I heard a voice in the midst of the four living creatures saying, A quart of wheat for a denarius, and three quarts of barley for a denarius; and do not harm the oil and the wine.

Things Prophesied

The third horseman to rule the Earth for Jesus was Great Britain, which was founded by King James who rode a black racing horse for which England is famous.

The British Empire is also famous for conquering with economics. It was the Brits who invented capitalism. And they formed and sent companies all over the world to exploit new lands and make money for the king. And they rarely had to fire a shot, and it is truly amazing. It is true that a quart of wheat for a denarius would have been a very expensive price for wheat in the first century, and some therefore say it indicates famine. But we should remember that Jesus is predicting prices in the 17th and 18th centuries, and the price does not indicate famine as much as it indicates inflation and the ability of the British to get top dollar for their products and services.

The Anglican Church which gave us the British Empire is represented by the third living creature which is said to be a man. It is probably meant to reflect, or signify, the enormous increase in man's knowledge during the reign of the British Church.

Both Canterbury and London (the Anglican lamp and stand) are pointed to by the star guide of Revelation 1 which guides the reader to all of the good things foretold.

The Fourth Horseman: A Literal Translation of Rev 6:7-8

And when He opened the fourth seal, I heard the voice of the fourth living creature saying, Come and see. [8]And I looked, and behold, a very pale [or sickly-looking] horse. And the name of him who sat on it was Death, and Hades was following him. And to him was given authority over the fourth of the earth, to kill with a sword, with hunger, with death, and by the beasts of the earth.

Things Prophesied

The fourth horseman to rule the Earth for Jesus is clearly the United States which was founded by George Washington who rode two different horses, but his favorite one was a rather pale-looking horse named "Blueskin." As for what his exact color was, most historians say he was bluish gray (or grayish blue) while one says he was white with a bluish tint. He is said to have been sired by a gray Arabian stallion called Ranger, and the breed of the mare is unknown. She was possibly a blue Nakota horse which is only found in the US (and originated in the Badlands of North Dakota, thus the name). But the name "Blueskin" suggests that he was born with a rare birth defect (that occasionally appears in humans and many other species) that turns skin a vivid blue. And blue skin is also a quite sickly looking color because many heart attack victims for example turn blue and soon die if they don't receive prompt medical attention. No other conqueror, before or since, has ever rode such a pale-looking horse.

It can truly be said that US weapons bring hell and death to the enemies of Jesus. And if it has not happened already, by the time the Battle of Ar Mageddon is over with (which began on 9/11), the US will most probably have brought hell and death to a fourth of the Earth (at least).

It should be noted that all of the horsemen of the Revelation are founded by a Church descended from St. Peter and the first century Church. That is, George Washington, like most of the US founding fathers, was an Episcopalian (the US branch of the Anglican Church which was founded in AD 47). And until Barack Obama, most of our presidents have been members of a Church descended from the first century Church established by St. Peter. It is the only Church that has been granted to rule the Earth for Jesus, and it can truly be said that the gates of hell cannot prevail against it.

Update: Donald Trump, it can be argued, is also a member of the established Church. That is, he is a member of the Presbyterian Church (as it is known in the US) which was established by the King of England much like the Anglican Church. Plus, he often attends the Episcopal Church where he and Melania got married, and where their son was baptized. Either way, it bodes well for the US.

The fourth horseman is introduced by the fourth living creature, the flying eagle, which also represents the United States on the dollar bill. The US Church, and especially the Episcopal Church which founded our great nation, truly brings peace in one hand and weapons in the other. The flying eagle also, according to Church tradition, represents St. Mark who founded the Anglican Church in AD 47, and it can be seen in many Episcopal/Anglican churches

The three historical capitals of the fourth horseman, New York City, Philadelphia and Washington D.C., are all pointed to by the starguide provided in chapter 1 that serves as a foolproof guide to all of the good things foretold in the Revelation. New York City is also the headquarters of the Episcopal Church (the lamp of the American lamp and stand, i.e., the Church and State).

What the future holds for the US

Unfortunately, the US (and the Episcopal Church) is now doing some things that are very likely displeasing to God (like performing same-sex marriages for example), and that will no doubt result in the fifth horseman arriving on the world scene. (In fact, he has already arrived—see commentary on chapter 19). And if Trump doesn't succeed in overturning Obergefell vs. Hodges (as promised), and also Roe vs. Wade (or if not entirely, at least stopping third-trimester abortions when the fetus is fully formed and capable of living outside the womb), then it will without a doubt be just a matter of time before God causes the United States to be surpassed by the fifth horseman as the most powerful nation on Earth.

Avenging the Martyrs: A Literal Translation of Rev 6:9-11

> And when He opened the fifth seal, I saw under the altar the souls of those who had been slain for the word of God and for the testimony which they held. [10]And they cried with a loud voice, saying, How long, O Lord, holy and true, until You judge and avenge our blood on those who dwell on the earth? [11]And a white robe was given to each of them; and it was said to them that they should rest a little while longer, until both the number of their fellow servants and their brethren, who would be killed as they were, was completed.

Things Prophesied

During the reigns of the four horsemen, many martyrs have been killed and have arrived in heaven (and especially in WW II). And they cry out and ask God (or Jesus) how long will it be until He avenges their blood on those who dwell on the Earth. They are told to wait until all the other martyrs are killed and join them in heaven. Then their deaths will be avenged.

Putting this vision together with the remainder of the Revelation, the inescapable conclusion is that the killing of the martyrs stops, and the avenging of their deaths begins, in the final battle between good and evil, variously known as Ar Mageddon, the Battle of that Great Day of God Almighty, and/or World War III. It is said, or signified, to begin at the start of the current millennium when the Euphrates is/was dry. And it did indeed begin in 2001 right on time, on 9/11, when also the lower fifty miles of the Euphrates was dry, having been dried up by Saddam Hussein (in 1992 or 1993).

Also, as soon as the Euphrates first went dry, the Bosniaks declared war on the Serbs, and the Serbs then avenged the slaughter of hundreds of thousands of Serbian martyrs over the centuries by killing 8000 of the Islamic enemies of Jesus—in the Srebronica Massacre. And while many Christian leaders may have condemned it, and still condemn it, it is one of the most highly praised events in all the Bible (see commentary on chapter 19). So the war in Bosnia, it can well be argued, was the opening salvo in the Battle of Ar Mageddon and in the avenging of the martyrs. (But a war is not a world war until the US is attacked and enters it).

Until very recently, "remember the martyrs" was the rallying cry of virtually all Christian armies since the days of Constantine. In Texas, we are famous for saying, "Remember the Alamo."

But today, it is not deemed by many Christians to be "politically correct" to say things like that. But the tide is turning, and the phrase is now coming back in Iraq—where we have indeed turned the tide, are now winning the war and avenging the deaths of thousands of US martyrs.

We can rest assured that there will come a day when there will be no more martyrdom, because Jesus says so. But it can only come to pass when we have avenged the martyrs and killed the last enemy of Jesus.

World War II: A Literal Translation of Revelation 6:12-17

And I saw when He opened the sixth seal, and behold, a great earthquake occurred, and the sun became black as sackcloth of hair, and the moon became like blood. [13]And the stars of heaven fell to the earth like a fig tree drops its late figs when it is shaken by a mighty wind.

[14]And the sky receded as a scroll when it is rolled up, and every mountain and island was moved out of its place. [15]And the kings of the earth, the great men, the rich men, the commanders, the mighty men, every slave and every free man, hid themselves in the caves and in the rocks of the mountains, [16]and they said to the mountains and to the rocks, Fall on us and hide us from the face of Him who sits on the throne and from the wrath of the Lamb! [17]Because the great day of His wrath has come, and who is able to stand?

Things Prophesied

In the Revelation, a great earthquake is a great worldwide war. It can well be argued that most everything in these verses is to be taken figuratively. World War II was the most earth-shaking and scariest war in the history of the world. But it can also be said that some of the things were fulfilled literally. WW II was indeed marked by a solar eclipse, a lunar eclipse, and meteor showers. Many islands and mountains changed hands. And many people hid as best they could.

The remaining seals, and the seven trumpet prophecies that follow, all expand on WW II.

The 144,000 Jews (Sixth Seal cont'd): A Literal Translation of Rev 7:1-8

After these things I saw four angels standing at the four corners of the earth, holding the four winds of the earth, that the wind should not blow on the earth, on the sea, or on any tree. ²Then I saw another angel ascending from the east, having the seal of the living God. And he cried with a loud voice to the four angels to whom it was granted to harm the earth and the sea, ³saying, Do not harm the earth, the sea, or the trees till we have sealed the servants of our God on their foreheads. ⁴And I heard the number of those who were sealed. One hundred and forty-four thousand of all the tribes of the children of Israel were sealed:

⁵Of the tribe of Judah twelve thousand were sealed;
Of the tribe of Reuben twelve thousand were sealed;
Of the tribe of Gad twelve thousand were sealed;
⁶Of the tribe of Asher twelve thousand were sealed;
Of the tribe of Naphtali twelve thousand were sealed;
Of the tribe of Manasseh twelve thousand were sealed;
⁷Of the tribe of Simeon twelve thousand were sealed;
Of the tribe of Levi twelve thousand were sealed;
Of the tribe of Issachar twelve thousand were sealed;
⁸Of the tribe of Zebulun twelve thousand were sealed;
Of the tribe of Joseph twelve thousand were sealed;
Of the tribe of Benjamin twelve thousand were sealed.

Things Prophesied

These verses are obviously referring to, or signifying, the 144,000 single male Jews who escaped death in the Great Tribulation of World War II by fleeing to Jerusalem. There, the history books tell us, they played a leading role in the founding of the new nation of Israel. One hundred thousand joined the new Israeli army, while forty-four thousand were conscientious objectors, that is, ultra-Orthodox Jews.

A Great Multitude Appears in Heaven: A Literal Translation of Rev 7:9-17

> After these things, I looked and behold, a great multitude, that no one could number, of all nations, tribes, peoples, and tongues, standing before the throne and before the Lamb, clothed with white robes, and with palm branches in their hands, [10]and crying out with a loud voice, saying, Salvation belongs to our God who sits on the throne, and to the Lamb! [11]And all the angels stood around the throne and the elders and the four living creatures, and fell on their faces before the throne and worshipped God, [12]saying, Amen! Blessing and glory and wisdom and thanksgiving and honor and power and might belong to our God to the ages of the ages.

> [13]And one of the elders answered, saying to me, Who are these arrayed in white robes, and where did they come from? [14]And I said to him, Sir, you know. And he said to me, These are the ones who come out of the great tribulation, and washed their robes and made them white in the blood of the Lamb. [15]Therefore they are before the throne of God, and serve Him day and night in His temple. And He who sits on the throne will dwell among them. [16]They shall neither hunger anymore nor thirst anymore, nor will the sun strike them, nor any heat, [17]because the Lamb who is in the midst of the throne shepherds them and He leads them to springs of waters of life. And God will wipe away every tear from their eyes.

Things Prophesied

These verses reflect the fact that fifty million people died in the greatest tribulation of all time known as WW II. Most of them were Christians, and they now wear robes of white in heaven, and join the four living creatures, the twenty-four elders and the angels in saying, Blessing and glory and wisdom and thanksgiving and honor and power and might belong to our God to the ages of the ages. Amen to that.

The Seventh Seal: A Literal Translation of Rev 8:1-5

And when He opened the seventh seal, there was silence in heaven for about half an hour. [2]And I saw the seven angels who stand before God, and seven trumpets were given to them.

[3]And another angel, who had a golden censer, came and stood upon the altar. He was given many incenses to offer, so that he could offer them with the prayers of the saints upon the golden altar before the throne. [4]And the smoke of the incenses, with the prayers of the saints, went up before God from the angel's hand. [5]And the angel took the censer, filled it with fire from the altar, and he threw it to the earth; and there occurred thunders, and voices and lightnings and an earthquake. [6]And the seven angels who had the seven trumpets prepared themselves to sound the trumpets.

Things Prophesied

These verses mainly introduce the angels with the seven trumpets which can be considered part of the seven seals which basically summarize the Revelation. In the chapters that follow, we get all the details.

It should also be noted that this scene reflects the teaching of the Orthodox and Roman Catholic Churches that our prayers should be offered with incense that carry our prayers to heaven. When they reach heaven, they sometimes result in an earthquake.

PART 4
The Seven Trumpets

Mark of the Beast, from canstockphoto.com

The First Trumpet: A Literal Translation of Rev 8:7

> And the first angel sounded his trumpet. And there occurred hail and fire mixed with blood, and they were thrown to the earth. And a third of the earth was burned up and a third of the trees were burned up, and all green grass was burned up.

Things Prophesied

The trumpet prophesies expand on the great tribulation of World War II. Hail and fire mixed with blood signify the bombs dropped in World War II on about a third of the Earth at the very least. And many trees etc. were burned up.

The Second Trumpet: A Literal Translation of Rev 8:8-9

And the second angel sounded his trumpet. And something like a great burning mountain was thrown into the sea, and a third of the sea became blood. ⁹And a third of the living creatures in the sea died, and a third of the ships were destroyed.

Things Prophesied

These verses signify the submarine warfare of WW II which destroyed approximately a third of the Earth's ships at the very least. Plus, sonar also kills fish.

The Third Trumpet: A Literal Translation of Revelation 8:10-11

And the third angel sounded his trumpet. And a great star fell from heaven, burning like a torch, and it fell on a third of the rivers and on the springs of water. ¹¹And the name of the star is called Wormwood. A third of the waters became wormwood, and many men died from the water, because it was made bitter.

Things prophesied

Wormwood is a plant noted for being very bitter. The one-third of the Earth aligned with Hitler became very bitter towards the Jews, and six million of them died from it. Hitler and his followers also became very bitter towards the Christian nations who came to their aid.

The Fourth Trumpet: A Literal Translation of Revelation 8:12-13

And the fourth angel sounded his trumpet. And a third of the sun was struck, and a third of the moon, and a third of the stars, so that a third of them were darkened. And a third of the day did not shine, and likewise the night.

¹³And I looked, and I heard an angel flying through the midst of heaven, saying with a loud voice, Woe, woe, woe to the inhabitants of the earth, because of the remaining blasts of the trumpet of the three angels who are about to sound!

Things Prophesied

The Revelation is still talking about the third of the Earth aligned with Hitler the anti-Christ. While some of that one-third of mankind may have called themselves Christians, they embraced and aligned themselves with darkness, not light.

The flying angel says "Woe, Woe, Woe" to the inhabitants of earth because of the three remaining blasts of the trumpet(s) about to sound.

The Fifth Trumpet: A Literal Translation of Rev 9:1-12

And the fifth angel sounded his trumpet. And I saw a star fallen from heaven to the earth. To him was given the key to the shaft of the abyss. [2]And he opened the shaft of the abyss, and smoke arose out of the shaft like the smoke of a furnace burning. And the sun was darkened, and the air, from the smoke of the shaft. [3]And out of the smoke locusts came forth to the earth. And power was given to them, as the scorpions of the earth have power. [4]They were commanded not to harm the grass of the earth, or any green thing, or any tree, but only those men who do not have the seal of God on their foreheads. [5]And they were not given authority to kill them, but to torment them for five months. Their torment was like the torment of a scorpion when it strikes a man. [6]In those days men will seek death and will not find it; they will desire to die, and death will flee from them.

[7]The shape of the locusts was like horses prepared for battle. On their heads were crowns of something like gold, and their faces were like the faces of men. [8]They had hair like women's hair, and their teeth were like lions' teeth. [9]And they had breastplates like breastplates of iron, and the sound of their wings *was* like the sound of chariots with many horses running into battle. [10]They had tails like scorpions, and there were stings in their tails. Their power was to hurt men five months. [11]And they had as king over them the angel of the bottomless pit, whose name in Hebrew is Abaddon, but in Greek he has the name Apollyon.

[12]One woe is past. Behold, yet two more woes are coming after these things.

Things Prophesied

The first "Woe" is the defeat of Moscow the Great Whore. She is described in chapter 17 as being briefly aligned with the anti-Christ and sitting on seven hills and many waters. That describes Soviet-era Moscow to a T. The first woe is known in the history books as the Winter War. John is talking about a shaft of cold air that stung the Soviet soldiers' toes like a scorpion for about 5 months. To John it may have looked similar to smoke from a furnace, but it was frost like smoke from a freezer. Abbadon and Appolyon are the equivalent of our Jack Frost.

The frostbite did not kill anyone, but it was so bad for about five months that it made the soldiers want to die. And in one of the greatest "Woes" of all time, little Finland stopped the westward advance of the Great Whore.

The star guide of chapter 1, provided by Jesus to guide us to all the good things foretold, very accurately points to the exact place where it happened.

The Sixth Trumpet: A Literal Translation of Rev 9:13-21

> And the sixth angel sounded his trumpet. And I heard a voice from the four horns of the golden altar which is before God, [14]saying to the sixth angel who had the trumpet, Release the four angels who are tied up at the great river Euphrates. [15]And the four angels, who had been prepared for the hour and day and month and year, were released to kill a third of men. [16]And the number of the troops of horses was two hundred million; I heard the number of them. [17]And thus I saw the horses in the vision and those who sat on them had breastplates of fiery red, and hyacinth blue, and sulfurous yellow/white. And the heads of the horses were like heads of lions; and out of their mouths came fire and smoke and brimstone. [18]By these three plagues a third of men were killed—by the fire and the smoke and the brimstone which came out of their mouths. [19]For their power is in their mouth and in their tails; for their tails are like serpents, having heads; and with them they do harm.
>
> [20]And the rest of men, who were not killed by these plagues, did not repent of the works of their hands, that they should not worship demons, and idols of gold, silver, brass, stone, and wood, which can neither see nor hear nor walk. [21]And they did not repent of their murders or their drugs or their fornication or their thefts.

Things Prophesied

First of all, we should note that there are only about fifty-eight million horses on the entire Earth, so it is impossible that these verses are talking literally about real horses. We should also note that sulfur has two colors. It is a dull yellow when cold, but it is a bright bluish-white when heated.

These verses are quite obviously talking about, or signifying, the great "Woe" known as D-Day, when close to two hundred million horses under the hood were unleashed against Hitler the Anti-Christ and the third of the Earth aligned with him. Those who sat on them are said to have insignias of red, white and blue—the colors which of course signify (primarily) the United States and/or US soldiers (even if a few smaller nations may use the same colors).

The two million horses ultimately led to Hitler's defeat and the end of the prophesied forty-two months of great tribulation. They were prepared, or manufactured, by four nations: Great Britain, Canada, Australia (remnants of the third horseman) and by the United States (the fourth horseman to rule the Earth for Jesus). The four nations are represented by the four angels. The English Channel is represented by the Euphrates River, the widest channel of water that John knew of.

Like all of the good events in the Revelation, the beaches of Normandy are very precisely pointed to by the star guide of Revelation 1.

But the killing off of Hitler and his forces did not cause the rest of mankind to repent of their evil ways. In fact, just the opposite has occurred. Since then, murders, drug-use, fornication, and thefts have all sky-rocketed.

The Seven Thunders (6th Trumpet, cont'd): A Literal Translation of Rev 10

And I saw a strong angel coming down from the sky, clothed with a cloud, and a rainbow on his head, and his face was like the sun, and his feet like pillars of fire, ²and he had in his hand an open scroll. And he put his right foot on the sea and his left foot on the land, ³and cried with a loud voice, as when a lion roars. And when he cried out, [it was like] the voice of seven thunders. ⁴And when the seven thunders spoke, I was about to write, and I heard a voice from the sky saying to me, Seal up the things which the seven thunders spoke, and do not write them.

⁵And the angel whom I saw standing on the sea and on the land raised up his hand to heaven ⁶and swore by the One living to the ages of the ages, who created heaven and the things in it, and the earth and the things in it, and the sea and the things in it, that there should be delay no longer, ⁷but in the days of the sounding of the trumpet of

the seventh angel, the mystery of God is finished, just as He declared the good news to His servants the prophets.

⁸And the voice which I heard from the sky spoke to me again and said, Go, take the little scroll which is open in the hand of the angel who stands on the sea and on the earth. ⁹And I went to the angel, saying to him to give to me the little scroll. And he said to me, Take and eat it; and it will make your stomach bitter, but in your mouth it will be as sweet as honey. ¹⁰And I took the little scroll out of the angel's hand and ate it, and in my mouth it was as sweet as honey. And when I had eaten it, my stomach became bitter.

¹¹And he said to me, You must prophesy again about many peoples, nations, tongues, and kings.

Things Prophesied

At first glance, there does not seem to be much of anything prophesied in this chapter. But that then begs the question, "Why would it be in the Revelation of the future if it does not reveal anything?"

A closer examination reveals that it may yet reveal a lot. That is, the seven thunders uttered by the mighty angel, with one foot in the sea and one foot on land, are said to have been sealed up by John. That means they are waiting to be found, and by sleuths in our generation equipped with a personal computer and software that can analyze the theometrics of the Revelation and spit out the exact spot to go to.

The Revelation gives us plenty of clues as to where they are. The position of the mighty angel, like the position of Jesus in the first vision, appears to be part of the theometry (or spherical geometry) woven into the Revelation. That is, he has his right foot in the sea, presumably the Aegean Sea which also marks the center of the first vision, and his left foot is on the Isle of Patmos, presumably where John is standing and where he sealed up the seven thunders. Like Jesus in the first vision, the angel is facing north, the orientation of any treasure map. By combining the two visions, an inquisitive reader of today, armed with a modern computer equipped with sophisticated spherical trigonometry software, should be able to easily go directly to the spot.

For now we can assume that the seven thunders have something to do with the sounding of the seventh trumpet, and the fulfillment of the seven last plagues that it ushers in which are said to finish everything. But they taste both bitter and sweet to John.

This chapter concludes with the angel telling John that he must "prophesy again about many peoples, nations, tongues, and kings." So the Revelation continues.

1260 Years of Trampling (6th Trumpet cont'd): Literal Translation of Rev 11:1-14

And I was given a reed like a measuring rod. And the angel stood, saying, Rise and measure the temple of God, the altar, and the ones worshipping in it. [2]But leave out the court which is outside the temple, and do not measure it, for it has been given to the nations. And they will tread the holy city underfoot for forty-two months. [3]And I will give power to my two witnesses, and they will prophesy one thousand two hundred and sixty days, clothed in sackcloth.

[4]These are the two olive trees and the two lampstands standing before the Lord of the earth. [5]And if anyone wants to harm them, fire proceeds from their mouth and devours their enemies. And if anyone wants to harm them, he must be killed in this manner. [6]These have power to shut up heaven, so that no rain falls in the days of their prophecy; and they have power over the waters to turn them to blood, and to strike the earth with every plague, as often as they may want.

[7]And when they are about to finish their testimony, the beast that ascends out of the abyss will make war against them, overcome them, and kill them. [8]And their dead bodies will lie in the street of the great city which spiritually is called Sodom and Egypt, where also our Lord was crucified. [9]And some of the peoples, tribes, tongues, and nations will see their dead bodies three-and-a-half days, and they will not allow their corpses to be put into graves. [10]And those who dwell on the earth will rejoice over them, make merry, and send gifts to one another, because these two prophets tormented those who dwell on the earth.

[11]And after the three-and-a-half days, the breath of life from God entered them—and they stood on their feet, and great fear fell on those who saw them. [12]And they heard a loud voice from heaven saying to them, Come up here. And they ascended to heaven in a cloud, and their enemies saw them. [13]In the same hour there was a great earthquake, and a tenth of the city fell. In the earthquake seven thousand people were killed, and the rest were afraid and gave glory to the God of heaven.

[14]The second woe is past. Behold, the third woe is coming quickly.

Things Prophesied

The only two worshippers that John finds in the temple of God—and the two olive trees, and the two lampstands, and the two witnesses who prophesy while Jerusalem is trampled by Gentiles—are quite obviously Christians and Jews, God's "chosen people." Everyone else is a "Gentile" (or unbeliever)

As for the 1260 days of trampling, in most Bible prophecies one day signifies one year. The prophesied 1260 years of trampling can be computed in either of two ways. First, it can be said to start with the conquest of Jerusalem by Omar around AD 636 or 637. He and his successors trampled Jerusalem until the end of World War I when the Ottoman Empire was defeated, except for a few years when the Crusaders ruled Jerusalem, and that computes to 1260 years. Alternately, it can well be argued that serious trampling of Jerusalem and the temple grounds did not begin until AD 685 when construction began on the Dome on the Rock, and the trampling did not end until the end of World War II when Jews came to be in the majority in the Holy Land. The second scenario also computes to 1260 years. Either way, it reveals (or signifies) that Muslims would be/were the seventh head of Satan to trample Jerusalem underfoot.

Historical accounts and tree rings reveal that during the 1260 years of trampling and prophesying, there was very little rain in the Holy Land, and the once fertile land turned into nearly a barren desert.

At (or near) the end of the 1260 years of trampling of Jerusalem by the seventh head of Satan, the eighth head of Satan (Hitler) appeared and killed millions of God's two witnesses, especially Jews, during precisely forty-two months of great tribulation—computed using the Hebrew 360-day sacred calendar used in Bible prophecies, and starting when the US entered the war (Dec 7, 1941, and ending with the death of Hitler (April 30, 1945).

Many people rejoiced and sent gifts to each other, etc., celebrating their dead bodies, especially in Berlin, the capital of the Third Reich of Rome where Jesus was crucified. But alas, a little over three years after World War II, on May 15, 1948, the Jews began to arise from the dead, so to speak, and launched their Revolution to take back the Holy Land. Then, in June 1949 the new nation of Israel launched "operation magic carpet," also called Operation on Wings of Eagles. Israel sent planes to Germany and throughout the world, and the pilots told all survivors of the holocaust who looked half-dead to "come up here," so to speak. And they ascended into heaven (or the sky), and flew to the Promised Land. Halfway between those two dates is 3 ½ years after WW II. And in that same hour (or year), seven thousand Jews died in the battle for Jerusalem and the Holy Land, and over 7000 Muslims.

Daniel's 70th week

Much of the Revelation is an expansion on (or explanation of) Old Testament prophecies. These verses are obviously an expansion on Daniel's seventieth week, with the first half being 1260 years, and not 1260 days as futurists would have you believe. The second half of the week is regular 24-hour days however. (See Daniel 9, but beware of mistranslations of ancient Hebrew into English.)

The Seventh Trumpet: A Literal Translation of Rev 11:15-19

And the seventh angel sounded his trumpet. And there were loud voices in heaven, saying, The kingdoms of this world have become the kingdoms of our Lord and of His Christ, and He shall reign forever and ever! [16]And the twenty-four elders who sat before God on their thrones fell on their faces and worshipped God, [17]saying,

We give You thanks, O Lord God Almighty,
The One who is and who was and who is to come,
Because You have taken Your great power and reigned.
[18]The nations were wrathful, and Your wrath has come,
And the time of the dead to be judged,
And to give Your reward to Your servants, and to the prophets and the saints,
And to those who fear Your name, to the small and to the great,
And to destroy those who destroy the earth.

[19]And the temple of God was opened in heaven, and the ark of His covenant was seen in His temple. And there were lightnings, noises, thunderings, an earthquake, and great hail.

Things Prophesied

These verses summarize the seven last plagues that follow, and the glorious one thousand year reign of twenty-four Christian elders (or kings, presidents and prime ministers) that they usher in. The saints and all who fear God's name both small and great will be rewarded, and those who destroy the Earth will be destroyed.

The Woman and Child (7th Trumpet, cont'd): A Literal Translation of Rev 12

And a great sign appeared in the sky; a woman clothed with the sun, with the moon under her feet, and on her head a crown of twelve stars. [2]And being pregnant, she cried out in labor and in pain to give birth.

³And another sign appeared in heaven: behold, a great, fiery red dragon having seven heads and ten horns, and seven diadems on his heads. ⁴His tail drew a third of the stars of heaven and threw them to the earth. And the dragon stood before the woman who was ready to give birth, to devour her Child as soon as it was born. ⁵She bore a male Child who was to rule all nations with a rod of iron. And her Child was caught up to God and His throne. ⁶And the woman fled into the wilderness, where she has a place prepared by God, that they should feed her there one thousand two hundred and sixty days.

⁷And war broke out in heaven. Michael and his angels fought with the dragon; and the dragon and his angels fought, ⁸but they did not prevail, nor was a place found for them in heaven any longer. ⁹And the great dragon was cast out, that serpent of old, called the Devil and Satan, who deceives the whole world; he was cast to the earth, and his angels were cast out with him.

¹⁰And I heard a loud voice saying in heaven, Now salvation, and strength, and the kingdom of our God, and the power of His Christ have come, for the accuser of our brethren, who accused them before our God day and night, has been cast down. ¹¹And they overcame him by the blood of the Lamb and by the word of their testimony, and they did not love their lives to the death. ¹²Therefore rejoice, O heavens, and you who dwell in them! Woe to the inhabitants of the earth and the sea! For the devil has come down to you, having great wrath, because he knows that he has a short time.

¹³And when the dragon saw that he had been cast to the earth, he persecuted the woman who gave birth to the male Child. ¹⁴And the woman was given two wings of a great eagle, that she might fly into the wilderness to her place, where she is nourished for a time and times and half a time, from the presence of the serpent. ¹⁵And the serpent spewed water out of his mouth like a flood after the woman, that he might cause her to be carried away by the flood. ¹⁶And the earth helped the woman, and the earth opened its mouth and swallowed up the flood which the dragon had spewed out of his mouth. ¹⁷And the dragon was enraged with the woman, and he went to make war with the rest of her offspring, who keep the commandments of God and have the testimony of Jesus Christ.

Things Prophesied

Here, there is very little of anything new prophesied, but it is a beautiful summary of all the events that have been prophesied in previous chapters, and of all of the important world events that have transpired since the birth of Christ.

The woman represents Mary in some ways, but it is better to think of the woman as Israel as a whole. Her baby is Jesus and also the Church. The seven-headed beast represents the seven heads of Satan to have ruled Jerusalem.

The sixth head, i.e., pagan Rome, tried to devour (or kill) Mary's baby on the day it was born. That is, on March 27, BC 4 when a bright Venus appeared over Bethlehem at high noon,[1] Jesus was born; and immediately the sixth head of Satan (King Herod, the governor appointed by Rome) tried to kill him; but it did not work. Again thirty-three years later, the sixth head of Satan (the Emperor himself) tried to kill Jesus, but again it did not work.

Jesus was caught up to heaven forty days later Luke tells us, and the Church He left on earth grew and flourished until AD 636-37 when the seventh head of Satan appeared on the scene in Jerusalem. That led to the woman (the Jews) fleeing into the wilderness (the rest of the world) for 1260 years— and some Christians also fled, who are Mary's (and Israel's) offspring.

Then, at the end of the 1260 years, the eighth head of Satan appears which is depicted as Satan himself cast down to Earth. The eighth head of Satan is of course Hitler who more than any other person in history persecuted the Jews, and he persecuted them like a flood for a time, times and half a time (three and one-half years). He also waged war with her offspring, the Christian nations that defended the Jews, and who keep the commandments of God and the testimony of Jesus the Messiah.

1. Source: *Distant Suns*, Ver. 2 (a star-tracking program for PCs)

The 8th Head of Satan (7th Trumpet cont'd): A Literal Translation of Rev 13

And I stood on the sand of the sea. And I saw a beast coming up out of the sea, having seven heads and ten horns, and on his horns ten crowns, and on his heads blasphemous names. [2]And the beast which I saw was like a leopard, his feet were like those of a bear, and his mouth like the mouth of a lion. And the dragon gave to him his power, and his throne, and great authority. [3]And I saw one of his heads as if it had been mortally wounded, and his deadly wound was healed. And all the world marveled and followed the beast. [4]And they worshipped the dragon who gave authority to the beast; and they worshipped the beast, saying, Who is like the beast? Who is able to make war with him?

⁵And a mouth was given to him speaking great things and blasphemies, and he was given authority to make war for forty-two months. ⁶And he opened his mouth in blasphemy against God, to blaspheme His name and His dwelling, and the ones who dwell in heaven. ⁷And it was granted to him to make war with the saints and to overcome them. And authority was given him over every tribe and people and tongue and nation. ⁸And all who dwell on the earth will worship him whose names have not been written in the Book of Life of the Lamb having been slaughtered from the foundation of the world.

⁹If anyone has an ear, let him hear. ¹⁰He who leads into captivity shall go into captivity; he who kills with the sword must be killed with the sword. Here is the patience and the faith of the saints.

¹¹Then I saw another beast coming up out of the earth, and he had two horns like a lamb and spoke like a dragon. ¹²And he exercises all the authority of the first beast in his presence, and causes the earth and those who dwell in it to worship the first beast, whose deadly wound was healed. ¹³He performs great signs, so that he even makes fire come down from heaven on the earth in the sight of men. ¹⁴And he deceives those who dwell on the earth by those signs which he was granted to do in the sight of the beast, telling those who dwell on the earth to make an image to the beast who was wounded by the sword and lived. ¹⁵He was granted power to give breath to the image of the beast, that the image of the beast should both speak and cause as many as would not worship the image of the beast to be killed. ¹⁶He causes all, both small and great, rich and poor, free and slave, to receive a mark on their right hand or on their foreheads, ¹⁷and that no one may buy or sell except one who has the mark or the name of the beast, or the number of his name.

¹⁸Here is wisdom. Let him who has understanding calculate the number of the beast, for it is the number of a man: His number is 666.

Things Prophesied

The first beast, that John sees coming up from the sea, at first has only seven heads. They are the seven heads of Satan (or pagan kingdoms) that have conquered Jerusalem over the course of history. The beast is a composite of all the beasts that Daniel said would conquer Jerusalem.

Then John sees a new head which is a resurrection of one of the original seven heads that was killed off and has now recovered from a mortal head wound. The Revelation is clearly talking about the Third Reich (of pagan Rome, which was the sixth head of Satan). The sixth head was originally killed off in AD 312 (by St. Constantine), and it can well be argued that it was again killed off in 1918 when the Second Reich of pagan Rome was defeated. The Third Reich of Rome was one man, Hitler, who was Satan personified. His Third Reich is the third head # 6 of the 666 trilogy.

The second beast, that John sees coming up from the earth, is a lamb with two horns. The lamb represents the Church, and the two horns are either the two Popes who backed Hitler (Pius XI and XII) or the two Churches which backed Hitler (the Roman Catholic Church and the Lutheran Church). It can truly be said that the two Popes and the two Churches are what gave Hitler his power. That is, they provided him with soldiers including the pilots who rained fire down from heaven, and they also gave Hitler their blessing which contributed to Hitler being worshipped. (Because everything in the Revelation has at least two meanings, both interpretations are valid).

World War II did not become a truly *world* war until the attack on the United States, and it lasted precisely forty-two months to the day, based on the 30-day months of the Hebrew sacred calendar used in Bible prophecies. In his book *"Mein Kampf,"* Hitler lays out his plan to prevent anyone from buying or selling food unless they have in their hand a permit stamped with a swastika or a swastika on their forehead (i.e, on their headgear). For the sake of the elect, those days were cut short (see Mat 24:22).

The Lamb & the 144,000 (7th Trumpet cont'd): Literal Translation of Rev 14:1-5

> And I looked, and behold, the Lamb standing on Mount Zion, and with Him one hundred and forty-four thousand having His Father's name written on their foreheads. [2]And I heard a voice from the sky, like the sound of many waters, and like the sound of great thunder. And the sound which I heard was the sound of harpists playing their harps, [3]and singing a new song before the throne, and before the four living creatures and the elders. And no one was able to learn the song except the hundred and forty-four thousand who were redeemed from the earth. [4]These are those who were not defiled with women, for they are virgins. These are those who follow the Lamb wherever He may go. These were redeemed from among men as firstfruits to God and to the Lamb. [5]And in their mouth was found no deceit, for they are blameless before the throne of God.

Things Prophesied

We should first note that the 144,000 standing on Mt. Zion with the Lamb only have His Father's name on their foreheads and not also His name—despite what some faulty translations may say.

They are the 144,000 single male Jews sealed from harm at the beginning of the Great Tribulation of World War II (see Revelation 7). They escaped harm by fleeing, unhindered by women or children, to the Holy Land. Some three and one-half years later, they played a leading role in founding the new nation of Israel where they raised the Star of David over Mt. Zion. The Star of David represents the Messiah which, of course, is Jesus. The 144,000 are said to learn a new song that only they can learn, and it will cause them to follow Jesus wherever He may lead. The redeemed Jews (saved from death) are said to be first-fruits to God and the Lamb. No deceit is found in their mouth, and they are deemed to be blameless before God.

But like most things in the Revelation, these verses appear to have a second meaning. It is difficult to find any data, but at the end of World War II, or in 1948, there were probably only about 144,000 Messianic Jews in the world. Now there are over a million of us, and it can well be argued that we will be the only ones able to learn the new song. It's not clear what all the new song entails, but it can be summed up as Messianic Judaism (which I'm a part of, and I will follow Jesus wherever He leads).

Three Proclamations (7th Trumpet, cont'd): A Literal Translation of Rev 14:6-13

And I saw an angel flying in mid-heaven, having the everlasting gospel to proclaim to those who dwell on the earth—to every nation, tribe, tongue, and people—[7]saying with a loud voice, Fear God and give glory to Him, for the hour of His judgment has come; and worship Him who made heaven and earth, and the sea and springs of water.

[8]And another, a second angel, followed, saying, Babylon has fallen, has fallen, that great city, because she has made all nations drink of the wine of the wrath of her fornication.

[9]And another angel, a third, followed them, saying with a loud voice, If anyone worships the beast and his image, and receives his mark on his forehead or his hand, [10]then he shall drink of the wine of the wrath of God, which is poured out undiluted in the cup of His wrath. And he shall be tormented with fire and brimstone before the holy angels and before the Lamb. [11]And the smoke of their torment ascends forever and ever; and they will have no rest day or night, who worship the beast and his image, and anyone who receives the mark of his name.

[12]Here is the endurance of the saints, the ones keeping the commandments of God and the faith of Jesus. [13]And I heard a voice from the sky saying, Write, Blessed are

the dead who die in the Lord from now on. Yes, says the Spirit, so that they may rest from their labors, and their works follow along with them.

Things Prophesied

The message of the first angel reflects the fact that shortly after World War II the Gospel was translated into virtually every language on Earth and flown to all the nations on Earth—thanks largely to the American Bible Society. The Gospel basically means Good News, but it also warns of the wrath of God who made heaven and Earth and demands our respect and worship or else we will receive His judgment.

The second angel announces the fall of Babylon. In the Revelation, Babylon is a term used for any non-Jewish, non-Christian conqueror of God's chosen people (the chosen people being Christians and Jews). In this case, the angel appears to be looking ahead a bit (to Rev 17), and is talking about the fall of Babylon the great whore who sits on seven hills and many waters, and is said to have been briefly aligned with the anti-Christ. That can only mean Moscow which sits on seven hills and five seas—thanks to the Moscow Canal. Plus Soviet-era Moscow was briefly aligned with Hitler at the start of World War II before he turned on her, exactly as prophesied. "A great whore" accurately describes a Christian nation that does an about face and embraces paganism or atheism. The Soviet Union, a Christian nation turned atheist, fell in 1991.

The third angel says anyone who worshipped Hitler (the anti-Christ), or worshipped his image (probably meaning the Aryan race), or wore the swastika on their forehead or in their hand, shall drink of the wine of the wrath of God, and be tormented by fire and brimstone in the afterlife. Verse 13 reflects the fact that Hitler killed many millions of Christians. Their works will follow them, and they will be blessed in the afterlife.

Reaping the Earth's Harvest: A Literal Translation of Rev 14:14-20

And I looked, and behold, a white cloud, and on the cloud sat One like the Son of Man, having on His head a golden crown, and in His hand a sharp sickle. [15]And another angel came out of the temple, crying with a loud voice to the One who sat on the cloud, Thrust in Your sickle and reap, for the time has come for You to reap, for the harvest of the earth is ripe. [16]And the One who sat on the cloud thrust in His sickle onto the earth, and the earth was reaped.

[17]And another angel came out of the temple which is in heaven, he also having a sharp sickle. [18]And another angel came out from the altar, who had power over the

fire, and he cried with a loud cry to him who had the sharp sickle, saying, Thrust in your sharp sickle and gather the clusters of the vine of the earth, for her grapes are fully ripe. [19]And the angel thrust his sickle into the earth and gathered the vine of the earth, and threw it into the great winepress of the wrath of God. [20]And the winepress was trampled outside the city, and blood came out of the winepress, up to the horses' bridles, for one thousand six hundred furlongs.

Things Prophesied

Mankind—or civilized man—has now reproduced and multiplied for six thousand years, and now the Earth is "ripe" and needs to be reaped. That is, the Earth being ripe signifies the fact that the Earth is now over-populated, and it is getting much worse every year and cannot continue. So Jesus (and/or two angels) are going to "harvest" it.

There appear to be two harvests foretold in these verses. If that is the case, the first harvest has to be World War II when fifty million people were killed.

The second harvest will be carried out through the seven last plagues and through the Church which has been treading the winepress of God's wrath ever since the second coming, in AD 312. In the seventh (and last) millennium of man's reign on Earth, God's wrath is pressed out by twenty-four Christian nations, chief of which will no doubt be Serbia which rules with a rod of iron and has already killed thousands of the enemies of Jesus—as we are commanded to do in Luke 19:27. The Srebronica Massacre is one of the most highly praised events in all the Bible (see commentary on Revelation 19). The United States has also done away with thousands of the enemies of Jesus (in Iraq and Syria), and it can well be argued that the US is behind most of the plagues. In summary, we are already witnessing the harvest(s) described here, and the reaping of humans will continue a while longer until the last plagues have run their course, and all the bad guys are dead.

PART 4
The Seven Last Plagues

The Scene in Heaven: A Literal Translation of Revelation 15

And I saw another sign in heaven, great and marvelous—seven angels having seven last plagues, because in them the wrath of God is completed. ²And I saw something like a sea of glass having been mixed with fire, and the ones prevailing over the beast, and over his image, and over his mark and over the number of his name, standing on the sea of glass, holding the harps of God. ³And they sang the song of Moses the servant of God, and the song of the Lamb, saying, "Great and marvelous are your works, Lord God the Almighty. Righteous and true are Your ways, O King of the nations. ⁴Who shall not fear You, Lord, and glorify Your name? Because You alone are holy. Because all nations will come and worship before You, because Your righteous judgments have been manifested.

⁵And after these things I looked, and behold, the temple of the tabernacle of the testimony in heaven was opened. ⁶And the seven angels went out from the temple, the ones having the seven plagues, who were dressed in pure bright linen, and girded around the chests with golden belts. ⁷And one of the four living creatures gave to the seven angels seven golden bowls filled with the wrath of God, the one living to the ages of the ages. ⁸And the temple was filled with the smoke from the glory of God and from His power; and no one was able to enter into the temple until the seven plagues of the seven angels were ended.

Things Prophesied

These verses follow the grim imagery of the fourteenth chapter where two figures with a sharp sickle harvest of the Earth (verses 14-21). The seven last plagues can be thought of as the actual means that the grim reapers use to harvest the Earth—that is, to bring widespread death. They are part of the wrath of God that is also foretold in the Gospels, which hint that half of the Earth (men and women) will be taken away in the last days (see Matthew 24:37-41 & Luke 17:34-37).

In the bigger picture, the seven last plagues can be considered part of the sounding of the seventh trumpet, which concludes the main body of the Revelation.

The Good News is, when the seven last plagues have run their course, the wrath of God is completed. Peeking ahead a bit, we find that they are followed by a glorious one thousand year reign of the Church (see chapter 20).

In verse 2, the figures seen standing on a sea of glass mixed with fire are those who have prevailed over the beast, that is, over the seventh and eighth heads of Satan which is Mohammed and Hitler, and all their devout followers. The "sea of glass mingled with fire" is apparently the same sea of glass that John saw in the second vision (in chapter 4), where he describes it as "a sea of glass like crystal." It appears to be a television or video screen of some sort, described in first-century terms.

The victors over the beast are playing harps and singing the same song that the twenty-four elders and the four living creatures are singing in chapter 5, "the Song of the Lamb".

Actually, the victors over the beast are here singing not just one song but two: "the Song of the Lamb" and "the Song of Moses" which seems to imply that both Jews and Christians are doing the singing.

The "Song of Moses" referred to is apparently the one Moses and the Hebrew slaves sang in Exodus 15:1-18. Basically, it celebrates the Hebrews' crossing of the Red Sea with the help of God, and then celebrates the wrath of God that consumed their Egyptian pursuers "like stubble". It concludes with "The Lord shall reign forever and ever" (compare with verse 7 of this chapter).

The "Song of the Lamb" references back to the new song of Revelation 5:9-10 that celebrates Jesus, the sacrificial Lamb and our redeemer, making us kings and priests to God. There, it is sung by twenty-four elders and four living creatures. The elders are wearing 24 crowns, which represent 24 Christian nations.

In the end when the seven last plagues have run their course, all who are left will fear God because of His righteous judgments and the whole world will worship Him. Many Churches today tend to only proclaim the love of God; but the Revelation reveals the wrath of God, and the need to fear God. In other words, God's love is a very tough love.

In the vision of the temple in heaven that follows (in verse 5), we should note that when the seven angels leave the temple in heaven, they do not yet have the seven bowls containing the last plagues, and they are given to them when they reach earth, by one of the four "living creatures."

The four living creatures are introduced in chapter 4, and they in turn introduce the four horsemen of chapter 6, the last one being the United States which currently rules the Earth for Jesus. Because the US Church is the de facto ruler of the Earth, and we are the earth's biggest polluter, it can well be argued we are responsible for most of the seven last plagues.

Verse 8 beautifully sums up the remaining events of the Revelation. The temple of God seen in heaven points to the glorious one thousand year reign of the Church on Earth that begins in chapter 20. It is heaven come to Earth, fulfilling the prayer Jesus taught us to pray, "Thy kingdom come on

Earth as it is in heaven." But we cannot enter into heaven on earth yet because of all the smoke from the seven last plagues. We will not be able to enter it until the seven last plagues have run their course and the smoke clears.

Skin Cancer: A Literal Translation of Rev 16:1-2

> And I heard a great voice from the temple saying to the seven angels, Go and pour out the bowls of the wrath of God on the earth. ²And the first went and poured out his bowl upon the earth; and an evil-looking diseased sore came upon the men who had the mark of the beast, and those who worshipped his image.

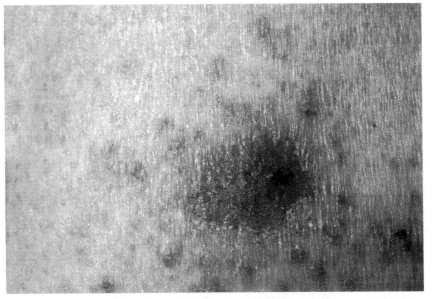

Skin Cancer, from shutterstock.com

Things Prophesied

The seven last plagues follow the great tribulation of World War II and the rebirth of Israel, in 1948. Shortly afterwards, the ozone layer started thinning, and cases of skin cancer started increasing, and soon began to skyrocket with millions of new cases every year. In verse 2, the grotesque imagery of evil-looking diseased sores quite accurately describes skin cancers.

We are told that this plague will plague surviving NAZIs and all those who worship the image that was worshipped by them (the Aryan race). A lot of NAZIs have experienced skin cancer and some have died from it—as have thousands of Aryans elsewhere, and especially those who worship the suntanned Aryan image which is popular today.

We should also note that in chapter 15, we are told that the plagues are handed to the seven angels by one of the four living creatures, presumably the flying eagle which represents the United States Church. This reflects the fact that the United States, with all our air conditioners, is/was the principle cause of the first plague. But we have since repented, and no longer use CFC's in our air conditioners, thank God.

Hopefully this plague will soon ebb. After all, virtually all NAZIs are now dead—except for maybe 3 or 4 who are hopefully about to be put on trial, and they will likely receive the death penalty if they do not die from old age before the trial is completed.

Red Tides: A Literal Translation of Revelation 16:3

> And the second angel poured out his bowl on the sea, and it became blood as of a dead man, and every living creature in the sea died.

Things Prophesied

The second plague is said to be red tides-the color of a dead man's blood—that kill all the fish in the sea. Nothing could describe the blooms of a class of algae, called dinoflagellates, any better. They are red and very deadly, and they turn the water into the color of a dead man's blood (see picture).

Red tides started increasing in the 1980's and are steadily increasing every year. Scientists say that at the rate fish are dying from red tides, and sometimes from green tides and often-colorless "dead zones" which keep growing bigger, all the fish in the sea will be dead by 2048.

Like skin cancer, red tides are apparently caused, at least in part, by man. That is, most scientists say red tides are escalating along our coasts mainly due to coastal water pollution containing the nutrients that algae blooms need, i.e., human sewage combined with fertilizer run-off from lawns and farms. They also say that global warming and rising sea temperatures—also caused by man—also plays a role. Another contributing factor, many scientists theorize, is that our tens of thousands of dams retain the needed sediment and cooler fresh water necessary for the survival of coastal marine life and the warding off of toxic algae. That means we need to repent, and stop interfering with the perfect way God created the Earth.

Here's what's currently happening in my neck of the woods (the Gulf of Mexico): This year, a mysterious blue-green algae bloom has been added to the deadly mix along the eastern coast (Florida's west coast). The source of it, *Synechococcus elongates*, is called "a kind of seaborne centaur." That is, like dinoflagellates, it is a one-celled half-plant/half-animal. Until very recently (about ten years ago), it had not been seen on Earth for approximately three billion years, scientists say. Now it has returned (probably due to the warmest seas in three billion years), and it has spread into virtually every sea, and in the Gulf it has now mutated into a very deadly form.[1] It deeply saddens me to say this, but with all the different forms and colorations of red tides now plaguing it, the Gulf of Mexico appears well on its way to becoming one of the first seas to bite the dust.

1.   From www.miaminewtimes.com/news/green-tide-6334640

Toxic Fresh Water: A Literal Translation of Rev 16:4-7

And the third angel poured out his bowl on the rivers and springs of water, and they became blood. [5]And I heard the angel of the waters saying, You are righteous, O Lord, the One who is, and who was and who is to be, because You have judged these things. [6]For they have shed the blood of saints and prophets, and You have given them blood to drink. They deserve it. [7]And I heard another from the altar saying, Yes, Lord God the Almighty, true and righteous are Your judgments.

Brain-Eating Amoebas, from shutterstock.com

Things Prophesied

This plague does not seem to be progressing quite as fast as the other plagues, at least in the United States and the developed world, but toxic drinking water is a major problem in the other half of the world where one-in-seven people do not have access to water from water-treatment plants as we have.

But even in the United States, this plague is starting to rev-up (and that implies, or signifies, that we have also shed the blood of the saints). Be that as it may, warmer water in our rivers and lakes—where most of our drinking water comes from—is now the breeding grounds of toxic stuff like algae blooms and a very scary new phenomenon, brain-eating amoebas. The brain-eating amoeba (Naegleria Fowleri) is very deadly and is increasingly appearing in US lakes and rivers, and in drinking water. There have been 37 reported cases in the ten years from 2006 to 2015, and 36 of the victims died (within 6 or 7 days usually). The amoeba has twice been found in New Orleans tap water, and in the tap water of several other cities. And earlier this year, there was also the lead poisoning in Flint, Michigan's tap water.

And drinking spring water won't save you either, according to the Revelation. And I predict that very soon the water from a famous spring, which has been safe to drink from for tens of millions of years, will turn very deadly to those who drink from it. My advice for 2017 is to stock up on distilled water (see "2017 in Bible Prophecy" on last page).

Global Warming: A Literal Translation of Rev 16:8-9

And the fourth angel poured out his bowl on the sun, and power was given to him to scorch men with fire. ⁹And men were scorched with great heat, and they blasphemed the name of God who has power over these plagues; and they did not repent and give Him glory.

Polar Bear on Disappearing Arctic Ice, from shutterstock.com

Things Prophesied

Being scorched by the sun is an excellent way to describe global warming. The planet began to gradually warm up in the 1980's, and it began to drastically warm up in the late 1990's; now it is fast accelerating every year. The year 2015 was by leaps and bounds the hottest year on record, breaking 2014's record heat by .29 degrees Fahrenheit; and 2016 is on track to break the 2015 record by an even greater margin.

Ninety-seven percent of scientists say this plague is mostly man-made and that the United States (represented by the fourth living creature) is the main culprit. Scientists fear that if nothing is done about the greenhouse gases that cause it, places like the Persian Gulf nations will soon be too hot for human survival. The recent Paris agreement should help mitigate it, but scientists predict that even if the goals of the Paris agreement are met, and global warming is held to two degrees Celsius, the melting of glaciers and the polar ice caps will continue for decades, and still raise sea levels by up to ten feet, flooding thousands of coastal communities. And they say that if our next president were to nix the agreement (as Trump once said he would do, but has now changed his mind, thank God) and nothing is done about greenhouse gases, sea-level will rise by up to twenty-two feet a hundred years or so down the road, putting half of Florida and all of Manhattan underwater. They also predict that global warming, when coupled with urban sprawl and the loss of wildlife habitats, will likely trigger the Earth's sixth mass extinction.

News reports in early March of this year were shocking. Across the northern hemisphere, the temperature, if only for a few days, crossed a line: it was more than two degrees Celsius above "normal" for the first time in recorded history and likely for the first time in tens of thousands of years.

That is important because the governments of the world have set two degrees Celsius as the must-not-cross red line which, theoretically, we are doing all we can to avoid. And it is important because most of the northern hemisphere did not have much of a winter season. They had to truck snow into Anchorage for the start of the Iditarod, and the normal Arctic sea ice on which polar bears and other wild life depend, was at record low levels for the wintertime. Additionally, in recent years the ice has disappeared almost entirely in the summer (see picture).

This plague is clearly accelerating and at a speed much faster than scientists had expected. August 2016 was the 16th consecutive month of record breaking temperatures.[1] The situation is dire because about half of the humans on Earth live within fifty miles of the sea, and it looks like about half of mankind may soon have to migrate somewhere because of global warming, especially when you factor in the equatorial nations that will soon be too hot for human survival. And that is provided they do not die first from this plague or one of the others.

Making a dire situation even worse, global warming is also producing bigger storms. The highest wind speeds ever measured came early this year in 2016 when Tropical Cyclone Winston crashed into Fiji. Entire villages were flattened. In financial terms, the storm wiped out ten percent of the nation's gross domestic product, roughly equivalent to fifteen simultaneous Hurricane Katrina's. Winston was followed by the highest wind speeds ever recorded in our hemisphere, when Hurricane Patricia crashed into the Pacific coast of Mexico.

In the latest news, the extinction of the first mammal due to human-caused climate change has been confirmed. It is (was) a small rat-sized mammal living on a small island in the Great Barrier Reef off Australia. Very little of the island remains visible today due to rising sea-level, and about one third of the corals of the Great Barrier Reef are also dead. And the rest are fast dying, which will no doubt cause the extinction of thousands of species of fish (part of last plague # 2). In other frightening news, carbon dioxide levels that Antarctica has not seen in four million years were just recorded, making it the last place on the planet to register the astounding concentration of the greenhouse gas now seen everywhere.[2]

We need to repent and begin taking drastic action if we want the Earth to survive and if we want to avoid destroying ourselves. We need to begin by closing down the "dirty" coal mines and power plants (by far the biggest culprit) because the idea of recapturing carbon from the smokestacks is not feasible at the present time, say most scientists and economists, because it would nearly double utility bills. It would also help if all of us were to install solar panels or windmills on our roofs (or both), and if all of us were to drive electric vehicles or take mass transportation, for other starters.

1. https://www.yahoo.com/news/earth-smashes-yet-another-heat-record-16th-month-175759429.html
2. Source: www.businessinsider.com

Atheism and New Diseases Increase: A Literal Translation of Rev 16:10-11

And the fifth angel poured out his bowl on the throne of the beast, and his kingdom became full of darkness; and they gnawed their tongues because of the pain. [11]And they blasphemed the God of heaven because of their pains and because of their ulcers, and did not repent of their deeds.

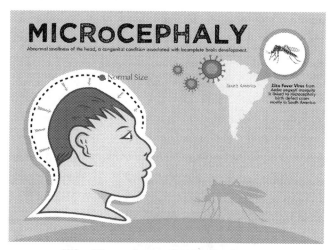

Zika Virus, from shutterstock.com

Things Prophesied

This plague, like the first one, seems to be primarily directed at the NAZIs who supported Hitler (the anti-Christ). And it can well be argued that in Germany, probably more so than in any other Christian nation, atheism has increased until most of the nation is living in darkness. But atheism is now increasing in most if not all Christian nations, so it also applies in a way to all Christian nations.

New diseases, i.e., new pains and ulcers, etc., are also increasing around the world, and especially in Brazil, where the Zika virus has appeared. New diseases that cause men to curse God include AIDS, MRSA, flesh-eating bacteria, Ebola, brain-eating amoebas, and now the Zika virus. Scientists theorize that the sudden outbreak of many new diseases are mutations of normally benign viruses and bacteria that are caused largely by global warming. Plus it is said that many doctors, especially in the United States, are causing the mutations of viruses by overprescribing antibiotics. In other words, the main cause of this plague, like most of the other plagues, appears to be man-made situations, with the US Church (the 4th living creature) being the primary enabler.

Brazil, the Revelation appears to be signifying, is the first nation to be plagued with the Zika virus because of the fact that at the end of World War II many Nazi's fled to Brazil to escape arrest and a fate of life in prison or death. The Brazilians turned a blind eye, but you cannot hide from God. In the Revelation, and throughout the Bible, there is a cause and effect for everything, even if it takes a few decades to play out.

On a personal note, Recife Brazil is where my ancestors hail from and where I still have distant cousins living in the heart (or epicenter) of this plague. I pray for all the Brazilians that this plague will not last much longer. On a brighter note, scientists have now found a way to kill off the Aedes mosquito that is at the source of the plague (with a device called CRISPR[1]), so it can happen. In short, this plague, like the first one, will probably begin to ebb once the last Nazi is dead. But on the other hand, Jesus tells us in the letter to Thyatira that He sometimes punishes the "bad guys" (and especially the "bad gals") to the second generation. So we will just have to try to avoid mosquitos in the meantime. And now the Aedes from Hades has reached Miami. My advice to all females who are either pregnant, or desire to be, is: Avoid Miami like the plague.

On another personal note, there are also some NAZIs (second generation) in my home town in Texas, so I'm pretty sure the Zika virus will be coming to Texas next (as scientists are also predicting). To try to avoid this plague, I'm stocking up on mosquito repellent now to avoid the rush. And I advise everyone on earth to do that in 2017 (see "2017 in Bible Prophecy" on last page). **Update:** The Aedes from Hades has now appeared in Texas just as I predicted.

1. CRISPR stands for Clustered Regularly Interspaced Short Palindromic Repeat. It is a device that allows scientists to easily and inexpensively find and alter virtually any piece of DNA in any species on earth from plants to animals. It is being used in Brazil to cause all of the male Aedes mosquitos to be sterile so that they cannot reproduce.

The Euphrates is Dried Up: A Literal Translation of Revelation 16:12-16

And the sixth angel poured out his bowl on the great river Euphrates, and its water dried up, so that the way of the kings from the east might be prepared. [13]And I saw three unclean spirits like frogs coming out of the mouth of the dragon, and out of the mouth of the beast, and out of the mouth of the false prophet. [14]For they are spirits of demons, performing signs, which come out on the kings of the whole inhabited earth to gather them to the Battle of That Great Day of God Almighty.

[15]Behold, I am coming as a thief. Blessed is he who watches, and keeps his garments, lest he walk naked and they see his shame.

[16]And they gathered them together to the place called in Hebrew, Ar Mageddon.

Dried-up Euphrates, from shutterstock.com

Things Prophesied

The lower fifty miles of the Euphrates was dry for at least ten years, from 1992 or 1993 until April 2003.[1] That means it was dry in 2001 at the start of the new millennium called That Great Day of God Almighty, when the great world-wide war (or great earthquake) known as Ar Mageddon is said to start. And that is precisely what happened, on 9/11.

As prophesied, the Euphrates was dried up (by Saddam Hussein) solely to prepare the way for the kings of the East in the Battle of Ar Mageddon (which is Islam's prophesied "Mother of All Battles" which ISIS, etc., believe they will win because the Koran says so). Hussein accomplished his feat with a couple dams and a diversion canal that he named "The Mother of All Battles River."

But no kings of the East actually crossed it, except maybe for Hussein. The "way" of the demon-possessed kings, it can well be argued, is the Jerusalem-Euphrates vector that very accurately points to the three kings who have started the Battle of Ar Mageddon. That is, a straight line drawn between Jerusalem and the epicenter of the dried up Euphrates (where it was dried up by Hussein), and then extended eastward, perfectly bisects Baghdad and Kabul and also Raqqa, the capital of ISIS.

The "kings" in Baghdad and Kabul have already been dethroned and killed and have been replaced with a new government. Now we are removing the demons from Raqqa. We have already killed a couple ISIS "kings", but they were immediately replaced with another; so we will have to step-up the plague of "exceedingly great hail" (plague # 7)—which Trump has promised to do—if we want to ever end the final battle for the earth.

But alas, when we extend the vector a bit further to the East, Tehran is next in line like four ducks in a row. Tehran was also identified by George W. Bush as being part of the "axis of evil." Another bad omen is that the Ayatollah, the real "king" of Iran, keeps flip-flopping on whether Iran should continue on its path to a nuclear bomb or bow to "Great Satan." His latest decision is to follow along with the president of Iran, and the United States, in order to lift economic sanctions. But the Ayatollah is growing old and will eventually die (as we all do), and chances are good that a "hardliner" will succeed him. Adding all the omens together, it looks as though we might have to also dethrone and kill Iran's king, or at least drop a few exceedingly great bunker-buster bombs on Iran's underground nuclear facilities. I am not officially predicting this (not wanting to make a self-fulfilling prophecy), but I am just saying what the bad vector woven into Revelation clearly points to, and it's a very bad omen.

The Euphrates was restored by Iraq's Marsh Arabs as soon as the United States toppled Hussein, on the day his statue fell. (So no one can say that George W. Bush did not do some good by invading Iraq.) Speaking of the US, this plague and the next one do not appear (at first glance) to have been started by the United States like the other plagues. But it can well be argued that "it takes two to tango", that the United States antagonized Hussein, and that it led to Hussein drying up the Euphrates and trying his best to start Ar Mageddon. Nonetheless, the US is not criticized in these verses.

Ar Mageddon means City(s) of the Sanctuary, and the Revelation is clearly talking about the original Sanctuary of God, the Garden of Eden (now Iraq and Syria) where God created the first man (or the first modern man, or civilized man). And it is also where the Euphrates dried up, and it can truly be said that virtually the whole world is now gathering to where it dried up, just as prophesied.

It should also be noted that the Euphrates has dried up at least two more times since Hussein dried it up. It was dry during 2008-2009, due in part to Turkey closing its new Grand Araturk dam, at the time the largest dam in the world, plus a two-year drought.[2] That is when the Iraqi Prime Minister said all United States ground troops must leave Iraqi which has proven to be a very bad decision.

It was dry again, or very nearly dry, in 2014 due largely to Turkey cutting off the flow of water again[3]—which is significant because that is when ISIS was born and invaded Iraq. The drying up of the Euphrates is truly a bad omen as prophesied, because every time it happens, something bad happens.

1. A University of Texas map, based on aerial photos of Iraq and dated June 1994, shows the lower fifty miles of the Euphrates as being completely dry. It is included in a CIA report titled, "*The Destruction of Iraq's Marshes*" (Report Number IA 94-10020).
2. Source: www.nytimes.com/2009/07/14/world/middleeast/14euphrates.html?_r=0
3. Source: www.thetrumpet.com/article/11828.19.0.0/middle-east/turkey-dries-up-the-euphrates

Battle of Ar Mageddon: A Literal Translation of Rev 16:17-21

And the seventh angel poured out his bowl into the air, and a loud voice came out of the temple of heaven, from the throne, saying, It is done! [18]And there were noises and thunderings and lightnings; and there was a great earthquake, such a mighty and great earthquake as had not occurred since men were on the earth. [19]And the great city came to be divided into three parts, and the cities of the nations fell. And Babylon the great was remembered before God, to give to her the cup of the wine of the rage of His wrath. [20]And every island fled, and mountains were not found. [21]And great hail, like hail weighing a talent, came down from the sky on men. And men blasphemed God because of the plague of the hail, because this plague was exceedingly great.

F-16 Loaded with "Exceedingly Great Hail" from shutterstock.com

Things Prophesied

The seventh plague is the Battle of Ar Mageddon, also called the Battle of that Great Day of God Almighty. Many dispensationalists have been saying for centuries (or millennia) that the Day of the Lord, or the Great Day of God Almighty, is the third millennium AD. While some mistakenly said it began in 2000, there is no year zero, so that means it actually began in 2001. And that is when the Revelation says (or signifies) the Battle of Ar Mageddon is to begin. And it did indeed begin in 2001, on 9/11, when it also happened that the Euphrates was dry. It has now escalated into a great worldwide war as prophesied.

"Ar Mageddon" is Hebrew for "City of the Sanctuary." A shortened form of the base word, "Megiddo" survives in most languages of the world today as "ghetto" which originally meant a sanctuary for the Jews, but now means any sanctuary for any race or creed. Going back still further, the word sanctuary originally referred to the Garden of Eden, the original sanctuary of God, fed by the Euphrates and Tigris rivers, and where He created man (or the first modern man, or *civilized* man).

And it is where the Euphrates was dried up by Saddam Hussein. The city (or cities) that lie at the epicenter of the great worldwide conflict now being waged on earth are Baghdad primarily, but also Damascus (also in the Garden of Eden). Both of them, plus all of Iraq and Syria, will very likely have to be split three ways to bring an end to the earth-shaking war in the Garden of Eden. (In the Revelation, a great earthquake is a great war).

The Good News is, the final battle between good and evil ultimately results in the latest face(s) of the seventh head of Satan (ISIS and Al Qaeda, et al.) being so soundly defeated (by a US-led coalition dropping "exceedingly great hail" on them) that Satan will not be heard from again for a thousand years.

With the Battle of Ar Mageddon, God's wrath is completed (although some of the last plagues like global warming may be with us for a while), and the long awaited glorious thousand year reign of the Church is able to begin.

But it may be several more months before the final battle between good and evil relents, so for 2017 I'm recommending that all Christians stock up on bullets, and if you don't own a gun, sell the shirt off your back and buy one (as Jesus commands us to do in Luke 22:36).

Moscow the Great Whore (last plagues cont'd): A Literal Translation of Rev 17

And one of the seven angels who had the seven bowls came and talked with me, saying to me, Come, I will show you the judgment of the great harlot who sits on many waters, ²with whom the kings of the earth committed fornication, and the inhabitants of the earth were made drunk with the wine of her fornication.

³And he led me away in the Spirit into a deserted place. And I saw a woman sitting on a scarlet beast filled with names of blasphemy, having seven heads and ten horns. ⁴The woman was arrayed in purple and scarlet, and adorned with gold and precious stones

and pearls, having in her hand a golden cup full of abominations and the filthiness of her fornication. ⁵And on her forehead a name was written:

MYSTERY, BABYLON THE GREAT,
THE MOTHER OF HARLOTS
AND OF THE ABOMINATIONS OF THE EARTH.

⁶And I saw the woman being drunk of the blood of the saints, from the blood of the witnesses of Jesus. And when I saw her, I marveled with great amazement.

⁷And the angel said to me, Why did you marvel? I will tell you the mystery of the woman and of the beast that carries her, which has the seven heads and the ten horns. ⁸The beast that you saw was, and is not, and is about to come up out of the abyss and go to perdition. And those who dwell on the earth will marvel, whose names are not written in the Book of Life from the foundation of the world, when they see the beast that was, and is not, and yet is.

⁹Here is the mind which has wisdom: The seven heads are seven mountains on which the woman sits. ¹⁰And there are seven kings. Five have fallen, one is, and the other has not yet come. And when he comes, he must continue a short time. ¹¹The beast that was, and is not, is himself also the eighth, and is of the seven, and is going to perdition. ¹²And the ten horns which you saw are ten kings who have received no kingdom as yet, but they receive authority for one hour as kings with the beast. ¹³These are of one mind, and they will give their power and authority to the beast. ¹⁴These will make war with the Lamb, and the Lamb will overcome them, for He is Lord of lords and King of kings; and those who are with Him are called, chosen, and faithful.

¹⁵And he said to me, "The waters which you saw, where the harlot sits, are peoples, multitudes, nations, and tongues. ¹⁶And the ten horns which you saw on the beast, these will hate the harlot, make her desolate and naked, eat her flesh and burn her with fire. ¹⁷For God has put it into their hearts to fulfill His purpose, to be of one mind, and to give their kingdom to the beast, until the words of God are fulfilled. ¹⁸And the woman whom you saw is that great city which reigns over the kings of the earth."

Things Prophesied

At first glance, this chapter seems to be a bit out of place because it talks mainly about events of World War II. But here John is expanding on the Great Whore, introduced in chapter 14, by saying something will happen to her—she will be judged—during the seven last plagues.

Moscow is the only city that sits on seven hills and many waters (five seas, thanks to the Moscow Canal). And Moscow was briefly aligned with Hitler the anti-Christ, and the ten nations aligned with him, before he turned on her. The many waters are also said to represent the many peoples, multitudes, nations, and tongues on which the whore sits, which fits Soviet-era Moscow to a T.

Two things have already happened to Moscow. First, in 1991, Soviet-era Moscow fell. And at the same time, the average life expectancy of Muscovites began to plummet downward—to 57, about thirty years less than the life expectancy of other industrialized nations. Things have improved a bit since then, but the life expectancy of Muscovites is still about twenty years less than in the West.

That, it could be argued, is punishment enough, but the next chapter seems to imply that Moscow will be one of three great cities that will be leveled by the "exceedingly great hail" dropped on the East by the US and its allies.

In the Revelation, a Great Whore can be defined as any Christian nation, or any Christian king or queen, that does an about face and converts to atheism or another religion. These verses may primarily refer to Moscow, but if we assume that definition also applies to princesses, then Princess Diana was also a great whore. And the minute she converted to Islam she was killed in the proverbial "bolt of lightning." God is like that sometimes.

As for the fate of Moscow, in the Revelation, the Euphrates is the boundary between the East (the "bad guys") and the West (the "good guys"). But Moscow straddles that boundary, half in the East and half in the West. When I fell asleep thinking about that perplexing quandary, I dreamed I was standing in Iraq looking at the dried up Euphrates. In the middle of it was a great whore, dying of AIDS and sitting in a wheelchair. Then a great curtain came down from heaven and separated the East from the West, and it caught the back of her wheelchair. She wanted to make it into the West, but she was stuck there in the middle of the Euphrates. So I ran, and with all the strength I could muster, I managed to pull her through into the West and into heaven (on Earth). But when I took a closer look at her, it turned out that the great whore was an ex-girlfriend of mine who would not remain true and loved to sleep around. So I am not sure what it all means.

But most of my dreams are prophetic, and right on the money. And as I often say, most things in the Revelation have three meanings. So what I think my dream means is, my ex-girlfriend (and I won't name any names to protect the guilty, but she knows who she is) was/is an example of a great Baptist whore (i.e., the church organist in a large Baptist church, and the best I have ever heard, who suddenly turned atheist). And I'm pretty sure she's going to die from AIDS or some other plague if she doesn't change her ways. But I now have some hope that I can pull her into heaven (after I pull Moscow into heaven with some help from Donald Trump).

So there you have it, three examples of a Great Whore (Russian, Anglican and Baptist, to prove I am an equal-opportunity offender), but with Soviet-era Moscow being by far the Greatest one.

Three Falls of Great Babylon: A Literal Translation of Rev 18

After these things I saw another angel coming down from heaven, having great authority, and the earth was illuminated with his glory. [2]And he cried mightily with a loud voice, saying, Babylon the great is fallen, is fallen, and has become a dwelling place of demons, a prison for every foul spirit, and a cage for every unclean and hated bird! [3]For all the nations have drunk of the wine of the wrath of her fornication, the kings of the earth have committed fornication with her, and the merchants of the earth have become rich through the abundance of her luxury.

[4]And I heard another voice from heaven saying, Come out of her, my people, lest you share in her sins, and lest you receive of her plagues. [5]For her sins have reached to heaven, and God has remembered her iniquities. [6]Render to her just as she rendered to you, and repay her double according to her works; in the cup which she has mixed, mix double for her. [7]In the measure that she glorified herself and lived luxuriously, in the same measure give her torment and sorrow; for she says in her heart, 'I sit as queen, and am no widow, and will not see sorrow.' [8]Therefore her plagues will come in one day—death and mourning and famine. And she will be utterly burned with fire, for strong is the Lord God who has judged her.

[9]And the kings of the earth who committed fornication and lived luxuriously with her will weep and lament for her, when they see the smoke of her burning, [10]standing at a distance for fear of her torment, saying, 'Woe, woe, the great city Babylon, that mighty city! For in one hour your judgment has come.'

[11]And the merchants of the earth will weep and mourn over her, for no one buys their merchandise anymore: [12]merchandise of gold and silver, precious stones and pearls, fine linen and purple, silk and scarlet, every kind of citron wood, every kind of object of ivory, every kind of object of most precious wood, bronze, iron, and marble; [13]and cinnamon and incense, fragrant oil and frankincense, wine and oil, fine flour and wheat, cattle and sheep, horses and chariots, and bodies and souls of men.

¹⁴The fruit that your soul longed for has gone from you, and all the things which are rich and splendid have gone from you, and you shall find them no more at all. ¹⁵The merchants of these things, who became rich by her, will stand at a distance for fear of her torment, weeping and wailing, ¹⁶and saying, Woe, woe, that great city that was clothed in fine linen, purple, and scarlet, and adorned with gold and precious stones and pearls! ¹⁷For in one hour such great riches came to nothing. Every shipmaster, all who travel by ship, sailors, and as many as trade on the sea, stood at a distance ¹⁸and cried out when they saw the smoke of her burning, saying, What is like this great city?

¹⁹And they threw dust on their heads and cried out, weeping and wailing, and saying, Alas, alas, that great city, in which all who had ships on the sea became rich by her wealth! For in one hour she is made desolate.

²⁰Rejoice over her, O heaven, and you holy apostles and prophets, for God has avenged you on her!

²¹And a mighty angel picked up a stone like a great millstone and threw it into the sea, saying, Thus with violence the great city Babylon shall be thrown down, and shall not be found anymore. ²²And the sound of harpists, musicians, flutists, and trumpeters shall not be heard in you anymore. No craftsman of any craft shall be found in you anymore, and the sound of a millstone shall not be heard in you anymore. ²³And the light of a lamp shall not shine in you anymore, and the voice of bridegroom and bride shall not be heard in you anymore. For your merchants were the great men of the earth, because by your sorcery all the nations were deceived. ²⁴And in her was found the blood of prophets and saints, and of all who were slain on the earth.

Things Prophesied

This chapter seems to be signifying three falls of great cities of Babylon, one in one day (or one year) and two in one hour (or one month). Babylon is a general catch-all term used throughout the Bible to refer to any pagan nation that attacks and kills God's Chosen people, Christians and Jews. But the original Babylon was in Eden, so the ISIS-held cities in Iraq and Syria doubly fit the bill.

But it is not clear whether the Revelation is also talking about Moscow, the Great Whore from the previous chapter or just three great cities in Iraq and Syria. Either way, the first great city to leveled by the "exceedingly great hail" dropped by US and NATO planes is definitely Ramadi. Nary a soul lives there anymore after nearly a year of constant bombing (or more than a year if the previous battles fought there are counted). As the Revelation says, "The light of a lamp shall not shine in you anymore."

Another great city of Babylon that is likely to be leveled soon is Raqqa—which President-elect Donald Trump has said he would do if elected. Bleeding-heart Christians need not fret. No innocents will be killed because ISIS has radicalized all their women and their children from the time they are toddlers, and those who disagree with ISIS fled the city long ago. **Update:** The latest news is that the ISIS fighters in Raqqa and Mosul are now planning to flee to "a fortress in the desert." If that is true, Trump will no doubt level it also.

It is too early to say with any certainty which city is the third great city that is destroyed by the plague of "exceedingly great hail," but Mosul, the last of the ISIS strongholds in Iraq, is one possible candidate. Aleppo, in Syria, is another great city that is on the verge of being destroyed and abandoned due to exceedingly great hail. Or it could be any of several smaller cities in Iraq and Syria that are already abandoned. Or it could (possibly) be Moscow (the Babylon of World War II), especially if the US were to attack Syria's president Assad (as many Democrats want to do), and Moscow comes to his defense as is bound to happen. (But it is not likely to happen now that Trump is the US President).

There once were many Christians in Iraq (in Ramadi, Fallujah, Mosul, etc.). In verse 4, Jesus is telling them to come out of Babylon lest they share in her plagues (i.e., the plague of "exceedingly great hail"). Most of them have already heeded the warning and have fled either to Kurdistan, or to Europe or to America.

If we assume that everything in the Revelation has two or more meanings, and two or more fulfillments, Kurdistan is another example of a new nation that no one else recognizes, except the Kurds (see Rev 2:17). Jesus seems to be telling Christians in Iraq (and in the US for that matter) to align themselves with the moderate Muslims in Kurdistan—as has indeed come to pass. And with the recent influx of Christians, together with the Christians who were already there, plus many new converts from Islam to Christianity in recent years, Kurdistan appears well on its way to becoming a new Christian nation in the Middle East. That has to be very pleasing to God.

Fifth Horseman & the Marriage Supper: A Literal Translation of Rev 19:1-10

> After these things I heard a loud voice of a great multitude in heaven, saying, Alleluia! Salvation and glory and honor and power belong to the Lord our God! [2]For true and righteous are His judgments, because He has judged the great whore who corrupted the earth with her fornication; and He has avenged on her the blood of His servants shed by her. [3]Again they said, Alleluia! Her smoke rises up forever and ever! [4]And the twenty-four elders and the four living creatures fell down and worshipped God who sat on the throne, saying, Amen! Alleluia! [5]Then a voice came from the throne, saying, Praise our God, all you His servants and those who fear Him, both small and great!

⁶And I heard, as it were, the voice of a great multitude, as the sound of many waters and as the sound of mighty thunderings, saying, Alleluia! For the Lord God Omnipotent reigns! ⁷Let us be glad and rejoice and give Him glory, for the marriage of the Lamb has come, and His wife has made herself ready. ⁸And to her it was granted to be arrayed in fine linen, clean and bright, for the fine linen is the righteous acts of the saints.

⁹Then he said to me, Write: Blessed are those who are called to the marriage supper of the Lamb! And he said to me, These are the true sayings of God. ¹⁰And I fell at his feet to worship him. But he said to me, See that you do not do that! I am your fellow servant, and of your brethren who have the testimony of Jesus. Worship God! For the testimony of Jesus is the spirit of prophecy.

Things Prophesied

John has repeatedly told us that with the seven last plagues, God's wrath is complete. And that means the Marriage Supper of the Lamb must also take place. It is said to follow the fall of Moscow the great whore (which occurred in 1991), and it marks the beginning of a glorious reign of Jesus and the Church. It is one of the most highly praised events in the Bible.

In verse 10, when John falls at the feet of the angel who tells him about the Marriage Supper of the Lamb, the angel tells him, Don't worship me, a fellow servant of Jesus—worship God, for the testimony (or proof) of Jesus is the spirit of prophecy. The latter is the main goal of this book—to prove to even the most hardened atheist that God (and Jesus) exist and are real through the spirit of prophecy.

Fifth Horseman & Marriage Supper (cont'd): Literal Translation of Rev 19:11-21

And I saw heaven opened, and behold, a white horse, and he who sat on it, called Faithful and True. And in righteousness he judges and makes war. ¹²His eyes were like a flame of fire, and on his head were many crowns having names written, and a name written that no one recognizes except himself. ¹³He was clothed with a robe dipped in blood, and his name is called The Word of God. ¹⁴And the armies in heaven, clothed in fine linen, white and clean, followed him on white horses. ¹⁵And out of his mouth proceeds a sharp double-edged sword, so that with it he might strike the nations. And he will shepherd them with a rod of iron. And he treads the winepress of the fierceness of the wrath of Almighty God. [16]And he has on his robe and on His thigh a name written: king of kings and lord of lords.

[17]And I saw an angel standing in the sun; and he cried out with a loud voice, saying to all the birds flying in the midst of heaven, Come gather together for the great supper of God, [18]so that you may eat the flesh of kings, and the flesh of captains, and the flesh of mighty men, and the flesh of horses and those sitting on them, and the flesh of all the people, both free and slaves, and both small and great.

[19]And I saw the beast, and the kings of the earth and their armies, gathered together to make war against him who sat on the horse and against his army. [20]And the beast was captured, and with him the false prophet who performed signs before him, by which he deceived those who received the mark of the beast and those who worshipped his image. These two were cast alive into the lake of fire burning with brimstone. [21]And the rest were killed with the sword proceeding out of the mouth of the one sitting on the horse, and all the birds were filled from their flesh.

Things Prophesied

Many Christians believe the fifth horseman is Jesus, but I disagree for many reasons—first of all because the history books (and Mat 24:30, Rev 1:7, etc.) tell us that Jesus returned in AD 312. But at the same time, it can well be argued that the five horsemen are five dispensations of the second coming.

John sees a horseman riding a white horse called "Faithful and True." That is, in verse 13, the name of the horseman is clearly said to be "The Word of God", and that leaves "Faithful and True" as the name of the horse. "Faithful and true" is the definition of "Orthodox," and it signifies that the fifth horseman rides the Orthodox Church into power, as did the first rider of the white horse.

The name of the fifth horseman, "Word of God," signifies that the fifth horseman is a Slav. That is, historians say "Slav" is short for "Slovo" which means "Word of God." The nation not recognized by anyone on Earth except the Slavs is without a doubt Republica Srpska.

Actually, only Serbia recognizes it. Therefore, the fifth horseman has to be Slobodan Milosevic and the Serbs. The president of Serbia is the "king" of the Serbian kings and lords. The collective Serbian white robe has been dipped in blood many times since 1389 when Satan's forces first attacked the Serbs and took Serbia (and Kosovo and Bosnia). The Serbs have retaken most of their homeland except for Kosovo. And they have retaken Kosovo from Satan's forces several times in many fierce battles since the dawn of the twentieth century and have shed a lot of blood in the effort. But the "powers that be" keep taking Kosovo away from the Serbs and giving it back to Satan's forces.

At times, Serbian martyrs have led the Serbs into battle as prophesied, wearing white robes and riding white horses—as is well documented by World War I historians. But the vast majority of the time since then, live Serbian priests, dressed in white robes, have led the Serbs into battle riding on the turret of a tank.

The sharp two-edged sword coming out of the horseman's mouth represents the Word of God by which he rules, judges, and makes war. It also signifies that the fifth horseman is one of the seven golden lampstands established by the early Church to give light to the seven parts of the Earth. When connected on a world map or globe, they form the blade of a sharp two-edged sword.

More so than any other Christian nation, the Serbs rule with a rod of iron. They truly tread the winepress of the fierceness of the wrath of God.

The Marriage Supper of the Lamb

As General Ratko Mladić said to the birds of the air, standing in the sun on the World News on virtually every channel on earth on the eve of the massacre he was about to carry out, the Srebronica Massacre was the prophesied Marriage Supper of the Lamb which results in thousands of corpses for the birds of the air to feast on. His exact words are quoted in Revelation 19:18. That may seem unchristian-like to some Christians, but in Luke 19:27 Jesus commands His followers to kill all His enemies—which He defines as anyone who does not want a Christian nation to rule over them. That fits the Srebronicans to a T. About half the Srebronicans' lives were taken, which fulfills the prophecy of Jesus in Luke 17:33-37 and Matthew 24:40-41. While some Christians may attempt to deny the obvious, this commentary will uphold the gospel truth, that the Srebronica massacre is one of the most highly praised events in all the Bible. We should be celebrating with the Serbs, and not condemning them for anything. And it was not a "genocide" because the Serbs let half the population live. And that's what Jesus wanted to happen, and while that may seem harsh, it's a bit of a change from the God of the Old Testament who sometimes told the Israelites, when they were conquering the Holy Land, to kill every last man, woman and child (e.g., see I Samuel 15:3). And to those who will probably argue that we are supposed to love our enemies, yes, we are supposed to love our personal enemies (as Luke 6:27 says), but we are also supposed to kill the enemies of Jesus (as Luke 19:27 says).

The Srebronica Massacre (or Marriage Supper) represents the proper marriage between Church and State. That is, in Republica Srpska, the Church and State are united as one. Also in Serbia, under Slobodan Milosevic, the Church and State were united as one. It is true that in 2000 he was defeated at the polls, was charged with war crimes and was sent to The Hague. The Good News is (or the really bad news for the enemies of Jesus is) Slobodan Milosevic's party is now back in power. Once again there is very little separation of Church and State in Serbia, and they function together as one as all marriages should—which is necessary if Christians are to conquer the world.

The False Prophet

The Muslim militants not killed by Slobodan Milosevic and his generals, plus the false prophet(s) who have aided the Islamic invaders of their homeland, "will be cast alive into the lake of fire burning with brimstone" (verses 20-21). It deeply saddens me to have to point to a popular fellow countryman, but Bill Clinton best fits the description of the false prophet. Almost single-handedly he enabled Muslims, the seventh head of Satan, to take over a Christian nation, i.e., Kosovo, which is a big "No-No" with God. It also saddens me that Bill Clinton has many followers today. I fear that we may all go to hell in a hand basket riding on Clinton's coattails (as the Revelation may be suggesting here) if things don't change. Also deserving mention is Britain, France, Germany and Italy, who voted with the United States to recognize the new Muslim/Satanic nation in Kosovo while at the same time refusing to recognize the new Christian nation in Bosnia (Republica Srpska).

The false prophet of this chapter should not to be confused with the two horned false prophet(s) of chapter 14 who backed Hitler in the 42 months of great tribulation known as World War II.

The Mark of the Beast

The mark of the beast of chapter 19 is most probably the Kosovo flag. John says anyone who receives it will be "thrown alive into the lake of fire burning with brimstone." The wording, "cast alive into the lake of fire" is most probably signifying a "living hell" as we often say today. That means all those who accept the Kosovo flag will experience living hell. (God says so, not me, so please don't get mad at the messenger).

The mark of the beast of this chapter should not be confused with the mark of the beast in chapter 14 which is the swastika.

Ar Mageddon

Last, but not least, it should be mentioned that the Srebrenica Massacre occurred shortly after the Euphrates went dry. That signifies that the Balkan wars are the opening salvo of the final battle between good and evil known as the Battle of That Great Day of God Almighty (also Ar Mageddon). It is the final battle between Christians and the seventh head of Satan, i.e., Muslim militants. In the first year of the New Millennium (on 9/11), it mushroomed into a World War as prophesied. (A war is not a *world* war until the United States gets attacked and enters it).

What the Future Holds for the Serbian Church, and for NATO

I believe Jesus (and God) is likely displeased with the United States (the fourth horseman) for several reasons, and over the next several decades (or centuries) God will cause the US to decrease in power, and cause the Serbs to increase in power until they are the most powerful nation on Earth. In the near future, the Serbs are on track to become the 24th Christian nation to join NATO (when the US Senate votes on it, probably in January, 2017), completing the picture of the 24 Christian thrones that will ultimately kill off the latest face(s) of Satan (i.e., Kosovo and Bosniak militants, ISIS and Al Qaida militants, all of them). The remaining NATO nations that are not wearing a wedding garment (as Jesus puts it in Mat 22:11-13) will be kicked out, and then Satan will not be heard from again for a thousand years—allowing the 24 Christian thrones to rule the Earth for Jesus unhindered by Satan for a millennium (see Rev 4:4 and Rev 20:4).

What the future holds for Gen. Ratko, and for the UN that put him in prison

It is true that General Ratko Mladic and his soldiers killed every male of fighting age, including even elderly men. That is also what King David did when he conquered the Holy Land (see I Kings 11, vv 14 & 23). It should also be noted that, despite what Muslims may claim, the old men were not "innocent old men." In fact, they were the evilest of the lot. That is, many of them were NAZIs who helped round up nearly 1 million Bosnian Serbs and send them to the gas chambers (along with many thousands of Jews they sent there). In addition, Gen. Ratko and his men also killed some female combatants. When you add up all the dead bodies, they amount to half of the population of Srebronica, just as signified in the Gospels (e.g., Luke 17:34-37).

Some people may not like it, but much of the Revelation is about avenging the death of the martyrs (e.g., see Rev 6:9-11), and that is no doubt a major reason why Gen. Ratko did what he did. For achieving that, while at the same time founding a new Christian nation, Gen. Ratko is one the most highly praised men in the Bible (along with King David who Jesus is descended from). Ratko Mladic (and his boss, RS president Radovan Karadzic) should not be in prison, and hopefully Donald Trump who loves Slavs/Serbs (his wife is one), will soon come to their rescue and (as he has already promised) overturn everything the Democrats have done in recent years, and (at some point) get them out. But that will no doubt necessitate the disbanding of the UN and its blasphemous "war crimes" tribunal. I have predicted that in "2017 in Bible Prophecy" (on the last page), but as I always say, I am sometimes a year or two ahead of God's timetable. When it does happen (with the help of the other 23 "politically incorrect" Christian leaders) God will indeed make the US (and the other Christian nations in NATO) great again as never before.

Regardless of what may happen on earth, Gen. Ratko and all other Christian soldiers who have conquered for Jesus and killed His enemies are guaranteed to receive a mansion in heaven (see John 14:2 and Rev 3:5) (And that includes us Viet Nam veterans despite what Jane Fonda, et al, may say).

For the latest updates on this section, go online to the7lastplagues.com

PART 5
The End

A Thousand Years of Heaven on Earth: A Literal Translation of Rev 20

And I saw an angel coming down from heaven, having the key to the bottomless pit and a great chain in his hand. [2]He laid hold of the dragon, that serpent of old, who is the Devil and Satan, and bound him for one thousand years; [3]and he cast him into the abyss, and closed and sealed it, so that he should not deceive the nations any more till the thousand years were finished. But after these things he must be released for a little while.

[4]And I saw thrones, and they who sat on them, and judgment was committed to them. Then I saw the souls of those who had been beheaded for their witness to Jesus and for the word of God, who had not worshipped the beast or his image, and had not received his mark on their foreheads or on their hands. And they lived and reigned with Christ for one thousand years. [5]And the rest of the dead did not come to life until the thousand years were finished. This is the first resurrection. [6]Blessed and holy is he who has part in the first resurrection. Over such the second death has no power, but they shall be priests of God and of Christ, and shall reign with Him one thousand years.

Things Prophesied

Up until this point, this commentary has mostly been a commentary on historical facts which are easy to write about and prove. Now comes the slightly harder part—predicting the future.

But with each passing day, the future becomes much clearer. Virtually every day, hundreds more of the last face of Satan (Islamic militants) are killed in Iraq and Syria and around the world. Soon, the last of Satan's forces will be so soundly defeated that He will not be heard from again for one thousand years. Then, twenty-four Christian thrones, as first prophesied in chapter 4, will be able to rule the earth unhindered by Satan for a millennium.

The Revelation is no doubt talking about NATO. A 24th Christian nation (Montenegro) is on track to be added to NATO in early 2017. At some point, the NATO nations not wearing a wedding garment (as Jesus puts it in Mat 22:12-13) will be kicked out.

The next thing that is said to happen is some beheaded martyrs will be resurrected from the dead. It is not real clear how that is going to come to pass. But the history books tell us that Jesus returned in AD 312, and it can well be argued that nowhere in the Bible does it say or signify that Jesus will return (in person) a third time. We can conclude therefore that it will likely be a feat performed by doctors.

In fact, we are already routinely raising people from the dead with CPR and defibrillators, etc. But verse 4 suggests a more impressive feat—either sewing someone's head back on, or (much more likely) bringing someone back to life who is brain dead.

We are fast arriving there. In 2011, a woman in a Catholic hospital in Manchester, New Hampshire was miraculously brought back from the dead after being legally dead for five hours—using a wonderful new machine called a cardiac bypass machine. More significantly, the US Department of Defense is now very heavily involved. In 2010, it launched a thirty-four million dollar initiative called Biochronicity. According to the Department of Defense, the battlefield application would be the slowing down or the stopping of time, making a wounded soldier able to survive longer—or even survive indefinitely—so that he can be transported somewhere to treat the injury, and then reverse that "suspended state" (between life and death).[1]

Plus, the Revelation also seems to indicate, or signify, that the first raising of the dead will happen on the battlefield, in the final battle between good and evil. If that is the case, the first resurrection of the dead will most probably take place in the US hospital in the Green Zone in Baghdad, in the epicenter.

As for humans being able to live to be a thousand years old, scientists say that is also inevitable with all the advancements in medicine and technology nowadays. Many scientists say that threshold will be reached by 2045.[2] I will go out on a limb here, and predict it will happen much sooner than that. With the advances being made in geriatrics and with the introduction, beginning in 2017, of CRISPR[3] technology that scientists say will soon lick cancer and pretty much every disease there is, I predict that a human born in 2017 will be the first to live to be 1000 years old (as some scientists are also saying[4]. One thing is for sure. It will happen, and happen soon, because Jesus said it will, and (as always is the case) Jesus and scientists agree 100 percent. They all say it is just a matter of *when* and not *if* or *maybe*.

1. *Popular Science*, July/August 2016, "The Re-animators" p. 54
2. *Scientific American*, September 2016, p. 72
3. CRISPR stands for Clustered Regularly Interspaced Short Palindromic Repeat. It is a device that allows scientists to easily and inexpensively find and alter virtually any piece of DNA in any species on earth from plants to humans. In 2017, it will be used for the first time (by Dr. Carl June at the University of Pennsylvania) to cure terminally ill cancer patients. Source: Time Magazine, Dec 19, 2016, p.116
4. For example, Dr Aubrey de Grey at the University of Cambridge is saying that. In fact, he says there is an 80% chance that someone born as early as 2015 will live to be 1000. Source: http://www.newsmax.com/SciTech/aging-researchers-immortality-Aubrey-de-Grey/2015/04/16/id/638926/

Satan Is Let Loose: A Literal Translation of Rev 20:7-10

And after the thousand years, Satan will be released from his prison. 8And he will come out to deceive the nations which are in the four corners of the earth, Gog and Magog, to gather them together to battle, whose number is as the sand of the sea. 9They went up on the breadth of the earth and surrounded the camp of the saints and the beloved city. And fire came down from God out of heaven and devoured them. 10The devil, who deceived them, was cast into the lake of fire and brimstone where the beast and the false prophet are. And they will be tormented day and night to the ages of the ages.

Things Prophesied

After one thousand years, Satan manages to make a comeback. He gathers all the nations from the four corners of the Earth, Gog and Magog, to make war against the camp of the saints. Then fire comes down from the sky and devours them. It is not clear who "them" is. Here the meaning seems to be that only the bad guys die, but the verses that follow suggest that everyone on Earth dies which suggests a great nuclear war which brings to pass the long-feared MAD (Mutual Assured Destruction).

The Battle with God and Magog a thousand years from now is also prophesied in Ezekiel 38.

The Great White Throne Judgment: A Literal Translation of Rev 20:11-15

And I saw a great white throne and Him who sat on it, from whose face the earth and the heaven fled away. And there was found no place for them. 12And I saw the dead, small and great, standing before God, and books were opened. And another book was opened, which is the Book of Life. And the dead were judged according to their works, by the things which were written in the books. 13The sea gave up the dead who were in it, and Death and Hades delivered up the dead who were in them. And they were judged, each one according to his works. 14Then Death and Hades were cast into the lake of fire. This is the second death. 15And anyone not found written in the Book of Life was cast into the lake of fire.

Things Prophesied

These verses imply that everyone on Earth dies in the big battle one thousand years from now. Then everyone is raised from the dead by God and judged in the great white throne judgment. In the final judgment, we are all judged according to our works—despite what many Churches teach. The Book of

Life, presumably a Church registry of sorts, is just one of several books opened. But anyone not found in the Book of Life will automatically be thrown into the lake of fire, probably the still-burning earth.

A New Earth and New Jerusalem: A Literal Translation of Rev 21

And I saw a new heaven and a new earth, for the first heaven and the first earth had passed away. And there was no more sea. [2]And I saw the holy city, New Jerusalem, coming down out of heaven from God, prepared as a bride adorned for her husband. [3]And I heard a loud voice from heaven saying, Behold, the tabernacle of God is with men, and He will dwell with them, and they shall be His people. God Himself will be with them and be their God. [4]And God will wipe away every tear from their eyes; there shall be no more death, nor sorrow, nor crying. There shall be no more pain, for the former things have passed away."

[5]And He who sat on the throne said, Behold, I make all things new. And He said to me, Write, for these words are true and faithful.

[6]And He said to me, It is done! I am the Alpha and the Omega, the Beginning and the End. I will give of the fountain of the water of life freely to him who thirsts. [7]The one that conquers shall inherit all things, and I will be his God and he shall be My son. [8]But the cowardly, and unbelieving, and abominable, and murderers, and fornicators and drug-users and idolaters, and all liars shall have their part in the lake which burns with fire and brimstone, which is the second death.

[9]And one of the seven angels who had the seven bowls filled with the seven last plagues came to me and talked with me, saying, Come, I will show you the bride, the Lamb's wife. [10]And he carried me away in the Spirit to a great and high mountain, and showed me the great city, the holy Jerusalem, descending out of heaven from God, [11]having the glory of God. Its radiance was like a most precious stone, like a jasper stone clear as crystal, [12]having a great and high wall with twelve gates, and twelve angels at the gates, and names written on them which are the names of the twelve tribes of the children of Israel: [13]on the east three gates, and on the north three gates, and on the south three gates, and on the west three gates.

[14]And the wall of the city had twelve foundations, and on them were the twelve names of the twelve apostles of the Lamb. [15]And he who talked with me had a gold reed to measure the city, its gates, and its wall. [16]And the city is laid out as a square,

and its length is as great as its breadth. And he measured the city with the reed at twelve thousand furlongs. Its length, breadth, and height are equal. [17]And its wall is one hundred and forty-four cubits, according to the measure of a man, that is, of an angel. [18]The construction of its wall was of jasper; and the city was pure gold, like clear glass. [19]The foundations of the wall of the city were adorned with all kinds of precious stones: the first foundation was jasper, the second sapphire, the third chalcedony, the fourth emerald, [20]the fifth sardonyx, the sixth sardius, the seventh chrysolite, the eighth beryl, the ninth topaz, the tenth chrysoprase, the eleventh jacinth, and the twelfth amethyst. [21]The twelve gates were twelve pearls: each individual gate was of one pearl. And the street of the city was pure gold, like transparent glass.

[22]And I saw no temple in it, for the Lord God Almighty and the Lamb are its temple. [23]The city had no need of the sun or of the moon to shine in it, for the glory of God illuminated it. The Lamb is its light. [24]And the nations of those who are saved shall walk in its light, and the kings of the earth bring their glory and honor into it. [25]Its gates shall by no means be shut by day, for night shall not exist there. [26]And they shall bring the glory and the honor of the nations into it so that they may enter. [27]And there shall by no means enter into it anything that defiles, or anyone causing an abomination or a lie, but only those who are written in the Lamb's Book of Life.

The New Jerusalem on dollar bill / canstockphoto.com

Things Prophesied

In the final judgment of everyone on earth, those found worthy get to go and live on a "new Earth without any sea," because the old Earth has passed away. The new Earth is no doubt Mars because that description fits the Mars terrain to a T. And for humans to be able to live on Mars, it would probably require a huge enclosed habitat like the New Jerusalem. It is made by God for the nations of those who are saved, i.e., Christian nations, and the Christian kings bring their glory into it.

God providing the light, like everything else in the Revelation, appears to have two meanings. God is there in person giving everyone light and knowledge, etc.; but the sun is somewhat dim on Mars, so God has to also provide the literal light that is necessary for life.

Two Trees of Life Bearing 24 Fruits: A Literal Translation of Rev 22:1-5

And he showed me a pure river of water of life, clear as crystal, proceeding from the throne of God and of the Lamb. ²In the middle of its street, and on either side of the river, was the tree of life, which bore twelve fruits, each tree yielding its fruit every month. The leaves of the tree are for the healing of the nations. ³And there shall be no more curse, and the throne of God and of the Lamb shall be in it, and His servants shall serve Him, ⁴and they shall see His face, and His name shall be on their foreheads. ⁵And night shall not exist, and there shall not be a need of a lamp or of light [from the sun], for the Lord God gives them light. And they shall reign to the ages of ages.

Things Prophesied

These verses describing the New Jerusalem appear to be mostly symbolic, but not entirely. It can well be argued that, like most everything in the Revelation, the river of water of life has two meanings. Either way, it is necessary to support life. It primarily represents Jesus and His teachings no doubt, but it also seems to indicate there is a river on Mars. And many scientists theorize that there is indeed an underground river on Mars, and that it can support life and possibly even a city the size of the New Jerusalem (if the water is conserved and recycled, etc.).

On either side of the river are two trees, and each one bears twelve different fruits. Their leaves are said to be for the healing of the nations, i.e., for the healing of the twenty-four different nations.

The square mileage of the New Jerusalem is significant. It happens to be precisely the square mileage (or square furlongs) of the territory conquered by St. Constantine at the second coming. It also accurately approximates the square mileage controlled by all the horseman. The jury is still out on the fifth horseman, but the second horseman (Roman Catholic Kings), the third horseman (the British Empire), and the fourth horseman (the United States) have each controlled close to two million square miles.

Not only does the Revelation suggest the United States is an early version of the New Jerusalem, but also on the back of the dollar bill, the US is represented by the New Jerusalem. There, it is depicted as a pyramid because our founding fathers, and most scientists, have deemed that in order for a structure the size of the New Jerusalem to support its own weight and be able to withstand earthquakes and storms, etc., it has to be pyramid-shaped.

The height of the New Jerusalem is also significant. It happens to be exactly the right height for a space elevator on Mars, which is necessary for easy travel (for God and humans?) between the stars.

Concluding Words: A Literal Translation of Rev 22:6-21

And he said to me, These words are faithful and true. And the Lord God of the holy prophets sent His angel to show His servants the things which must shortly take place.

[7]Behold, I am coming quickly! Blessed is he who keeps the words of the prophecy of this book.

[8]Now I, John, saw and heard these things. And when I heard and saw, I fell down to worship before the feet of the angel who showed me these things.

[9]And he said to me, See that you do not do that. For I am your fellow servant, and of your brethren the prophets, and of those who keep the words of this book. Worship God. [10]And he said to me, Do not seal the words of the prophecy of this book, for the time is at hand. [11]He who is unjust, let him be unjust still; he who is filthy, let him be filthy still; he who is righteous, let him be righteous still; he who is holy, let him be holy still.

[12]And behold, I am coming quickly, and My reward is with Me, to give to everyone according to his work. [13]I am the Alpha and the Omega, the Beginning and the End, the First and the Last.

[14]Blessed are those who do His commandments, that they may have the right to the tree of life, and may enter through the gates into the city. [15]But outside are dogs and

sorcerers and sexually immoral and murderers and idolaters, and whoever loves and practices a lie.

¹⁶I, Jesus, have sent My angel to testify to you these things in the churches. I am the Root and the Offspring of David, the Bright and Morning Star.

¹⁷And the Spirit and the bride say, Come! And let him who hears say, Come! And let him who thirsts come. Whoever desires, let him take the water of life freely.

¹⁸I testify to everyone who hears the words of the prophecy of this book: If anyone adds to these things, God will add to him the plagues that are written in this book. ¹⁹And if anyone takes away from the words of the book of this prophecy, God shall take away his part from the Book of Life, from the holy city, and from the things which are written in this book.

²⁰He who testifies to these things says, Surely I am coming quickly. Amen. Even so, come, Lord Jesus! ²¹The grace of our Lord Jesus Christ be with you all. Amen.

Wrapping up the Revelation

In the concluding words of the Revelation, Jesus says three times that He is returning quickly. To say He did not is to call Jesus a liar. And Jesus does not lie, so that means all who deny the second coming (in AD 312) are the liars and in danger of being shut out of the New Jerusalem lest they repent.

In verse 16, Jesus tells us He is the Bright Morning Star. Also called the Star of David by the Jews, the Bright Morning Star represents the Messiah from the line of David who is to rule the world. Also, a bright morning star (the star in the East) marked the birth of Jesus as recorded in Matthew. The appearance of Venus over Bethlehem during an eclipse can easily be seen with any star-tracking software set to high noon on March 27, BC 4. Since the second coming, in AD 312, Jesus has indeed ruled the world—through the Church.

In verse 18, John concludes the Revelation by adding a curse on anyone who takes away from, or adds to, the Revelation. In this commentary on the Revelation, I have taken special pains not to do that. Comparing the Revelation to historical and scientific facts is not adding to the Revelation. It is what Jesus wants us to do in order to prove to even the most hardened atheist that He is real and His words are true.

2017 in Bible prophecy

As any scientist will tell you, the ultimate proof of any theory even eschatological ones
is their ability to accurately predict things
For many hundreds of years, many hundreds of futurists have made hundreds of predictions
and never have they been able to accurately predict things

I have been making predictions for 25 years now and they always come true
Though I will admit I am sometimes ahead of God's timetable by a year or two
And I typically add something like the end is near
This year I'm saying the end is here!

1. The EU will disband, and also the UN and some of NATO
And a new world order will spring up out of the ashes
And then the Church will rule the earth for Jesus
For a glorious thousand years or so.

2. The seven golden lampstands of the Church will unite again
In the restoration of all things,
And the Church will once again be able to roar like a lion
And rid the earth of evil things.

3. The plagues of red tides, toxic fresh water, global warming, and new diseases
Will probably continue for a while until the wrath of God eases,
But the plagues of skin cancer and the Zika virus will begin to be abated
When the last NAZI, and the Aedes from Hades, are eradicated.

4. It may be several months before the final battle between good and evil relents,
So I suggest stocking up on can goods, distilled water, mosquito spray and bullets.

5. The Good News is, the first resurrection of a "beheaded martyr"* is performed by Medics,
And Trump and other "politically incorrect" Christians will rule the earth's politics.
Plus someone born this year will live to a thousand with the advances in geriatrics!
* Or brain-dead martyr

Your kingdom come, your will be done on earth as it is in heaven, Amen!

Barry Midyet

Printed in the United States
By Bookmasters